TWAYNE'S WORLD AUTHORS SERIES

A Survey of the World's Literature

YIDDISH

Isaac Bashevis Singer

TWAS 582

Isaac Bashevis Singer

ISAAC BASHEVIS SINGER

By EDWARD ALEXANDER

University of Washington

TWAYNE PUBLISHERS

A DIVISION OF G. K. HALL & CO., BOSTON

Published in 1980 by Twayne Publishers,
A Division of G. K. Hall & Co.
All Rights Reserved

Printed on permanent/durable acid-free paper and bound
in the United States of America

Library of Congress Cataloging in Publication Data

Alexander, Edward.
Isaac Bashevis Singer.

(Twayne's world authors series ; TWAS 582)
Bibliography: p. 155–57
Includes index.
1. Singer, Isaac Bashevis, 1904–
—Criticism and interpretation.
PJ5129.S49Z57   839'.09'33   79-21272
ISBN 0-8057-6424-0

שמע לאביך זה ילדך

ואל תבוז כי זקנה אמך

Proverbs 23:22

Contents

About the Author

Edward Alexander was born in Brooklyn, New York, in 1936. He received his B.A. from Columbia (where he was elected to Phi Beta Kappa) in 1957, his M. A. from Minnesota in 1959, and his Ph.D. from Minnesota in 1963. He has taught at the University of Washington in Seattle since 1960, and is now Professor of English and Chairman of the Jewish Studies Program there. He was a Visiting Professor at Tufts University in 1968. In 1961 he was awarded a Fulbright Fellowship to London University, in 1966 an American Council of Learned Societies Fellowship, in 1974 a John Simon Guggenheim Fellowship, and in 1975 a fellowship from the National Foundation for Jewish Culture.

Professor Alexander is best known for his books and essays on Victorian literature. He is the author of *Matthew Arnold and John Stuart Mill* (Columbia University Press, 1965), *John Morley* (Twayne, 1972), and *Matthew Arnold, John Ruskin, and the Modern Temper* (Ohio State University Press, 1973). He is also the editor of *John Stuart Mill: Literary Essays* (Bobbs-Merrill, 1967). He has published many essays and reviews on the Victorians in *University of Toronto Quarterly, Modern Language Review, Journal of English and Germanic Philology, Dickensian, Victorian Poetry, Victorian Studies, Victorian Newsletter, American Historical Review,* and *Queen's Quarterly.*

In the area of Jewish Studies he has recently published a book entitled *The Resonance of Dust: Essays on Holocaust Literature and Jewish Fate* (Ohio State University Press, 1979). His essays and reviews on Jewish subjects have appeared in *Midstream, Judaism, Commentary,* and *Alternative: An American Spectator.*

Preface

This study of Isaac Bashevis Singer considers him as what he has often said he is, "a writer in the Jewish tradition but not exactly the Yiddish tradition." I believe that Singer exists for a large part of his readership in what Cynthia Ozick has called New Yiddish, a Jewish dialect of English in the way that "Old" Yiddish was a Jewish dialect of Middle High German. Singer has facilitated the creation of this literary hybrid by working very closely with his translators. Indeed, Singer himself does most of the translation into English from the point of view of Yiddish, so that these "translators" are in most cases more like collaborators or editors. Singer takes the work of translation with utmost seriousness, and has said that "to me the translation becomes as dear as the original." The works studied in this book, then, are those by which Singer has chosen to make himself known to the English reader, those that have earned him his international reputation and the Nobel Prize for Literature. I have omitted discussion of works never translated into English and therefore little known beyond a small and rapidly diminishing audience— albeit an audience that makes up in quality what it lacks in quantity. I have also left out of consideration Singer's books for children, despite their great distinction and wide popularity.

Even in English translations, many Yiddish and Hebrew words are left untranslated by Singer. For this reason, I have provided a brief glossary of terms frequently used instead of translating them each time they appear in the text.

My primary emphasis is on Singer the novelist. Each of the chapters from 2 through 8 is devoted to one of the novels, which are treated according to their order of publication. The chapter on Singer's first novel, *Satan in Goray*, has been expanded to allow for a brief account of the Sabbatian movement of the seventeenth century, which plays so large a role in Singer's subsequent work. Chapter 9 deals, all too briefly, with the short stories.

I have incurred several debts, which I am happy to acknowledge, in the course of writing this book. The primary one is to my wife, Leah Alexander, who first introduced me to Singer's work, and revealed to me that the study of English literature had become a distraction so great that it did not allow me to reflect on that from which I had been distracted. I am indebted to the National Foundation for Jewish Culture and the John Simon Guggenheim Foundation for fellowships which allowed me time to work on this book. For typing the manuscript I am indebted to the secretarial staff of the University of Washington Department of English, and especially to Jane Cornell, who is at once typist and editor. For her drawing of Singer, I am indebted to Rebecca Frieda Alexander.

I would like to give the following acknowledgments: Selections from A CROWN OF FEATHERS by Isaac Bashevis Singer. Copyright © 1970, 1971, 1972, 1973 by Isaac Bashevis Singer. From GIMPEL THE FOOL by Isaac Bashevis Singer. Copyright © 1953, 1954, 1955, 1957 by Isaac Bashevis Singer. From IN MY FATHER'S COURT by Isaac Bashevis Singer. Copyright © 1962, 1963, 1964, 1965, 1966 by Isaac Bashevis Singer. From THE FAMILY MOSKAT by Isaac Bashevis Singer. Copyright 1950 by Isaac Bashevis Singer. Renewed Copyright © 1978 by Isaac Bashevis Singer. From THE MAGICIAN OF LUBLIN by Isaac Bashevis Singer. Copyright © 1960 by Isaac Bashevis Singer. From THE MANOR by Isaac Bashevis Singer. Copyright © 1967 by Isaac Bashevis Singer. From SATAN IN GORAY by Isaac Bashevis Singer. Copyright 1955 by Isaac Bashevis Singer. From THE SEANCE AND OTHER STORIES by Isaac Bashevis Singer. Copyright © 1964, 1965, 1966, 1967, 1968 by Isaac Bashevis Singer. From SHORT FRIDAY by Isaac Bashevis Singer. Copyright © 1961, 1962, 1963, 1964 by Isaac Bashevis Singer. From SHOSHA by Isaac Bashevis Singer. Copyright © 1978 by Isaac Bashevis Singer. From THE SLAVE by Isaac Bashevis Singer. Copyright © 1962 by Isaac Bashevis Singer. From THE SPINOZA OF MARKET STREET by Isaac Bashevis Singer. Copyright © 1958, 1960, 1961 by Isaac Bashevis Singer. From ENEMIES, A LOVE STORY by Isaac Bashevis Singer. Copyright © 1972 by Isaac Bashevis Singer. From THE ESTATE by Isaac Bashevis Singer. Copyright © 1969 by Isaac Bashevis Singer. Reprinted by permission of Farrar, Straus and Giroux, Inc.

EDWARD ALEXANDER

University of Washington
Seattle, Washington

Chronology

appears in *Partisan Review* and introduces Singer to non-Jewish audiences.

1955   *Satan in Goray* appears in English translation, by Jacob Sloan.

1957   *Shadows on the Hudson* serialized in the *Forward*. Publication of first collection of short stories in translation, *Gimpel the Fool and Other Stories*.

1958   *A Ship to America* published serially in the *Forward*.

1959   *The Magician of Lublin* serialized in the *Forward*.

1960   *The Magician of Lublin* published in English translation.

1961   *The Spinoza of Market Street.*

1962   *The Slave.*

1964   *Short Friday and Other Stories.* Elected to National Institute of Arts and Letters.

1966   *In My Father's Court* (an autobiographical memoir).

1967   *The Manor* (written between 1953 and 1955).

1968   *The Seance and Other Stories. When Shlemiel Went to Warsaw and Other Stories* (Children's Book).

1969   *The Estate.*

1970   *A Day of Pleasure* wins National Book Award for Children's Books. *A Friend of Kafka and Other Stories.*

1972   *Enemies, A Love Story.*

1973   *A Crown of Feathers and Other Stories.*

1974   National Book Award. *The Penitent* (Yiddish only).

1975   *Passions and Other Stories.*

1978   *A Young Man in Search of Love. Shosha.* Receives Nobel Prize for Literature.

CHAPTER 1

Between Religion and Worldliness: A Literary Vocation

I am happy to call myself a Jewish writer, a Yiddish writer, an American writer.

—Isaac Bashevis Singer, Acceptance
Speech for 1974 National Book
Award in Fiction

ISAAC Bashevis Singer was born on July 14, 1904, in Leoncin, Poland, the third child of Bathsheva (née Zylberman) Singer and Pinchos-Mendel Singer. He was born into that world of almost medieval Jewish orthodoxy which no longer exists in Europe, and of which there are only traces left in Israel and the United States today. His father was an impoverished rabbi and Chasid, his mother the descendant of rabbis equally pious but more inclined to the rationalistic tradition of Chasidism's opponents, the *misnagdim*. Singer's wish consciously to appropriate his mother's rationalistic strain as well as his father's mystical intensity is indicated by his decision to add the name "Bashevis" to his given name in signing his published works (which in Yiddish bear only the name "Isaac Bashevis").

Yet if one were to search out the unique contribution of his upbringing to his literary genius, that trait which he could hardly have acquired anywhere else in the modern Jewish world, it would have to be his father's unworldliness. By Pinchos-Mendel's unworldliness we are to understand not merely his (apparently stubborn) refusal to be examined in Russian and pay court to the local governor so that he could be named (he never was) an official rabbi, and not merely his unwavering conviction (which, says Singer, he himself later came to share) that "the 'world' itself was *tref* [unclean],"[1] but his willingness to believe in the mystical and the su-

13

pernatural. By the early twentieth century, the Jews of Europe, who had traditionally defined and disciplined themselves by the understanding that they had been chosen to receive the Law, were becoming skeptical of God but enthralled by the varieties of anthropomorphic idolatry known as liberalism, humanism, and enlightenment. That is to say, the Jews were becoming a worldly people, a people that denied its own transcendent reason for being. "Worldliness," says Cynthia Ozick, is "the gullibility that disbelieves everything."[2] Singer is almost guilty of understatement in remarking, in his memoir of his father's rabbinical court, that "even at that time, such unworldliness was rare."[3]

It was a function of Singer's father's unworldliness to treat theater, art, and literature as idolatrous and tending in the direction of apostasy. The wearing of masks was objectionable; the painting or sculpting of images was clearly a violation of the second commandment. Literature might at first seem less offensive because it was, like Jewish religion itself, oriented toward the word, toward speech. But in fact Pinchos-Mendel Singer saw in literature, and especially Yiddish literature, the most potent threat of all:

My father used to say that secular writers like Peretz were leading the Jews to heresy. He said everything they wrote was against God. Even though Peretz wrote in a religious vein, my father called his writing "sweetened poison," but poison nevertheless. And from his point of view he was right. Everybody who read such books sooner or later became a worldly man and forsook the traditions. In my family, of course, my brother had gone first, and I went after him. For my parents, this was a tragedy.[4]

Yet we know that Singer's parents despaired prematurely, for their younger son did not, like his artist-novelist brother Israel Joshua, become a completely "worldly man." His relationship to Chasidic materials is not the same as that of Peretz, the writer who aroused the rabbi's wrath. Peretz placed himself at a distance from a system of belief which he admired and praised but could not share. Singer, although far less confident than Peretz had been of the moral efficacy of Chasidism, implicitly acknowledges the authenticity of passionate religious belief and contemns skepticism as a foolish prohibition of questioning in the face of phenomena which materialism and "common sense" cannot fathom.

The rabbi's hostility to Yiddish literature was but one aspect of his revulsion from what later came to be called, however illogically, "secular Jewishness." Peretz and his friends wanted to "liberate" the Jews from orthodoxy, but not to make them into Gentiles. His hope was to continue the ancient tradition, but in a secularized form. The Zionists aspired to very much the same thing, but looked to Hebrew and Palestine rather than Yiddish and Poland as their instruments. But for Pinchos-Mendel all departures from piety were ultimately the same, and ultimately frivolous: "The neighborhood teemed with Zionists, socialists, territorialists, assimilationists. Yiddish and Hebrew secular literature already existed, but to Father, all of this non-Jewishness signified nothing."[5]

Given his father's views, it is hardly surprising that Singer's education was encompassed by the boundaries of Jewish religion. It was an education both broad and profound, with the Bible at its center providing the life-giving sap to those branches and fruits known as Midrash, Talmud, Responsa, Kabbalah, and so on endlessly. But it drew up short at the frontier of modern secular knowledge, which was essentially the knowledge of the Gentile world. A literature written in Hebrew figures that imitated the literature of the Gentiles, a political movement like Zionism which produced a Jewish version of Gentile nationalism—what were these but halfway houses on the way toward worldliness? Singer recalls how in Warsaw "Father himself never stepped out on the balcony, except on very hot summer evenings, when the heat indoors was unbearable. The balcony was already a part of the street, of the crowd, of the Gentile world and its savagery."[6]

The first in the family to venture into this world was Isaac's elder brother Israel Joshua, who violated nearly all his father held sacred by becoming, first an artist, then a writer, and then a soldier in the Czar's army: the logical progression, the old man must have thought, for one who had chosen the path of Esau. Even Singer's mother, who was "a marvelous storyteller,"[7] reacted to the horrifying spectacle of her two sons scribbling and sketching with the reproof: " 'Normal children don't act that way.' "[8]

Israel Joshua became a devotee of the Jewish Enlightenment. Even while still wearing Chasidic garb, he regaled his mother with the truths flowing in upon him from Copernicus, Newton, and Darwin. It is clear from Singer's account of his brother's enlightened and progressive zeal that Israel Joshua is the prototype for that legion of characters in the novels who berate the Jews for their Oriental backwardness and refusal to join in the progressiveness of the European march of intellect. " 'Mother,' " Israel Joshua would shout, " 'you can see what Jews look like—stooped, despondent, living in filth. Watch them drag their feet as they walk. . . . Listen to them speak. It's no wonder everyone else thinks of them as Asiatics. And how long do you think Europe will stand for this clump of Asia in its midst?' "[9] Ironically, when the First World War broke out, Israel Joshua was led, by his "modern" and enlightened ideas, to join the army of the Czar instead of following the traditional Jewish modes of evasion.

Although Israel Joshua introduced his brother to many ambiences and experiences which belonged to the regimen of the "enlightened," he does not seem to have inculcated in him the doctrines of enlightenment. In 1914 Israel Joshua gave Isaac his first secular book, Dostoevsky's *Crime and Punishment* (in Yiddish translation). In order to carry food from his parents to the son who had left them for "the world," young Isaac had to frequent the artist's studio which had become his brother's residence. Here he discovered that there were some circles in which the body was respected more than the soul, in which it was assumed that "there was more to a boy than the ability to study," and in which women bared their breasts for purposes other than nursing babies. Through the agency of his brother,

the ways of the intelligentsia became more familiar to me. They neither prayed nor studied from holy books nor made benedictions. They ate meat with milk, and broke other laws. The girls posed nude with no more shame than they would have about undressing in their own bedrooms. In fact, it was like the Garden of Eden there, before Adam and Eve had partaken of the Tree of Knowledge. Although they spoke Yiddish, these young people acted as freely as Gentiles.[10]

Some of all this was bound to have its effect upon a young mind previously cut off from the world. Even before he became *bar mitzvah* Isaac Singer was afflicted with doubt and developing a taste for heresy. But at no time does he appear to have accepted his brother's doctrinaire idealization of the ways of the "emancipated." The new experiences altered his perspective but did not succeed in uprooting him or making him turn traitor to what had previously nurtured him. His brother's studio, to be sure, "was quite a change from my father's studio, but. . . this pattern has become inherent to me. Even in my stories it is just one step from the study house to sexuality and back again. Both phases of human existence have continued to interest me."[11] So far as religious practice was concerned, the cheder, the study house, and his father's courtroom were beginning to lose their hold on Singer, but they had permanently captured his imagination.

The Singer family had lived in Warsaw, in very straitened circumstances, since 1908. In a sense, they were among their neighbors but not of them. "Although mother and father were not much alike, both were revolted by vulgarity, boastfulness, conniving, and flattery. . . . We were the inheritors of a heroic code. . . the essence of which was an ability to endure suffering for the sake of spiritual purity. But all around us seethed a rabble who did not share our ideals."[12] In 1917, when he was thirteen, Isaac and his mother went to Bilgoray, where they would live for four years, formative ones for the budding writer. Bilgoray was removed both in time and space from the corrosive influences of modernity. At first young Isaac was frustrated by a place so entirely without the worldliness of Warsaw. Heretical books were unavailable, and he soon felt that he had been "condemned to antiquity." Eventually, to be sure, he discovered that "the evil spirit. . . had a small following even in Bilgoray":[13] that is to say, there were a few Bundists, a few Zionists, a few enlighteners. To outward view, Singer himself appeared to add to their number by becoming a writer of Hebrew poems and stories and a teacher of Hebrew in a "worldly" school for the boys and girls of Bilgoray. It was also in Bilgoray that he fell under the influence of the writings of the arch-heretic Spinoza, an influence from which he did not liberate himself for many years.

But the really formative influences of Bilgoray upon Singer were coming from other sources altogether and working largely unconsciously. It was precisely Bilgoray's "antiquity," that which the progressives and enlighteners wished to improve out of existence, that provided Singer with the imaginative and spiritual nourishment which has sustained him to this day. "In Bilgoray I was able to witness holiday celebrations that had not changed for centuries. . . . In this world of old Jewishness I found a spiritual treasure trove. I had a chance to see our past as it really was. Time seemed to flow backwards. I lived Jewish history."[14] Singer has remarked that he could never have written *Satan in Goray* or other works set in the seventeenth century if he had not lived these four years in a town which had hardly changed since the time of Chmielnicki's massacres. But Bilgoray, in what his brother would have called its "Asiatic" stationariness, was also to become for Singer an abiding symbol of the destroyed life of European Jewry once the Nazis had completed their murderous work.

In 1921, Singer, unwilling to move with his mother, father, and younger brother to another *shtetl* in which his father had received a rabbinical post, agreed to enroll in the Tachkemoni Rabbinical Seminary in Warsaw. This was the price he had to pay to return to worldly life in the big city. But he left the seminary, which he hated, after about a year and returned briefly to Bilgoray, where he again took work as a Hebrew teacher. By 1923, however, he was back in Warsaw, committed to the literary life and trying to support himself as a proofreader for *Literarishe Bletter*, the Yiddish literary magazine.

The closest we have to a full account of Singer's apprenticeship as a Yiddish writer in the Warsaw of the 1920s is his memoir entitled *A Young Man in Search of Love* (1978). Here Singer tells of his libertine existence, of his elderly mistress, Gina, of his long campaign to elude the clutches of the Polish army, of the agonies, the sheer physical torment of spending hour after hour proofreading versified propaganda. Inevitably, he found himself frequently in the company of "emancipated" Jews who combined an enormous yearning for worldliness with "a boundless energy."[15] Yet this energy usually flowed into activities which either bored or horrified Singer. Whereas the traditional Jew had fought with himself, "with that power of Evil that roosts in every brain and constantly strives to lead it astray,"[16] the modern Jew strove to conquer only external enemies, and in the process of combating the injustices of the world was corrupted by them. Singer's experiences of Jewish Warsaw during the 1920s convinced him that Enlightened Jews had become the chief idolaters of modern Europe.

Yet Singer himself was under the sway of what Irving Howe has called the one genuine contribution of the Jewish Enlightenment to Yiddish literature: "simply the *idea* of writing—that is, the idea that a secular career as a writer was worthy of a mature Jewish intelligence."[17] Troubled though he was by the doubtful future of the Yiddish language, resentful as he was of the tradition that a Yiddish writer must be not merely an artist but a defender of his people, distressed as he was by his own elder brother's public assertion that to write in Yiddish was to debase oneself as an artist,

Singer was undeterred from his vocation. Nothing shows better his severe dedication to his craft and his entire indifference to the idle winds of literary and political fashion than his decision to set his first novel, begun in 1933, in seventeenth-century Poland. Refusing to descend to the "relevance" which was demanded and narrowly defined by all the leftists in Yiddishist circles, he adhered to his belief that truth was to be found not in philosophy, psychology, and sociology, but in folklore, dreams, and fantasies. Sophisticated readers, to be sure, must have recognized that the deranged Messianism which Singer took as his subject in *Satan in Goray* was by no means the exclusive possession of the seventeenth century.

In 1935, Israel Joshua Singer, now a successful writer (and in the language he once despised) in New York, brought his younger brother to the United States. Isaac became a free-lance writer with *Der Forverts* (The Forward), thus forming an association which is unbroken to this day. But his creative work languished, and indeed he appears almost to have been struck dumb by what America revealed to him about the future of Yiddish:

When I came to this country I lived through a terrible disappointment. I felt then—more than I believe now—that Yiddish had no future in this country. In Poland, Yiddish was still very much alive when I left. When I came here it seemed to me that Yiddish was finished: it was very depressing. The result was that for five or six or maybe seven years I couldn't write a word. Not only didn't I publish anything in those years, but writing became so difficult a chore that my grammar was affected. I couldn't write a single worthwhile sentence. I became like a man who was a great lover and is suddenly impotent, knowing at the same time that ultimately he will regain his power. [18]

This case of amnesia, which Singer has often called the one illness Jews are *not* afflicted with, may be traceable to external causes—the impending destruction of the whole Yiddish-speaking population of Europe, the elevation of Hebrew above Yiddish in the *yishuv* in Palestine, the flight of Jewish Americans from the language of their parents—but the causes of its cure are much more elusive, for the passage of time exacerbated rather than alleviated the sickness of Yiddish.

By 1943 Singer's creative vein had once again begun to flow. *Satan in Goray* was reissued in this year along with five new stories, among them the excellent tales "The Destruction of Kreshev" and

"Zeidlus the First." In the same year he became a regular contrib-
utor to the *Forward*, where he was henceforth to publish his popular
journalism under the name of Isaac Warshofsky (the man from
Warsaw), and his serious literary work under the name of Isaac
Bashevis (with the name Singer reserved for his translated works).
In 1945, as if continuing a genre in which his recently deceased
brother Israel Joshua had excelled, Singer commenced the long
family saga, *The Family Moskat*, published serially in the *Forward*
through 1948 and then published in book form in 1950. This great
novel was translated into English, with the active involvement (as
has been the case with all subsequent translations of his work) of
the author himself, and sold 35,000 copies, giving Singer for the
first time a glimpse of the huge audience which awaited him outside
of the Yiddish world. In 1953, Saul Bellow's publication of his own
translation of "Gimpel the Fool" in *Partisan Review* gave Singer's
work the imprimatur of the high priests of literary modernism and
helped to gain for his work an acclaim beyond what any Yiddish
writer had ever received in non-Yiddish literary circles.

Since that time Singer has gone from triumph to triumph. His
productivity—short story after short story, novel after novel—has
been enormous, exceeded among American writers of the first rank
perhaps only by William Faulkner. He has been honored with every
major literary award. After two decades of abject poverty, he has
become prosperous as well as famous and is reported to earn over
$100,000 a year from advances, royalties, lecture fees, and motion
picture and television options on his work.[19] The adulation and
rewards of the world have not caused Singer to swerve from his
stubborn integrity as a writer determined to go his own Jewish way.
In a sense, his lonely dedication to Yiddish has been vindicated,
although at a terrible price. For the virtual disappearance of the
Yiddish world has made it easier for Yiddish literature to remain
Jewish in content and form than it is for modern Hebrew literature,
whose younger Israeli practitioners strive mightily to be "like the
nations." As recently as 1976, Singer said that he was "shocked to
see modern Hebrew literature becoming more and more worldly."[20]
If it seems ungracious for a writer who has been so well treated by
the world to be so contemptuous of its standards, we must remember how cruel was the irony whereby Yiddish literature, in the
person of Singer, should have received the high honor of a Nobel

Prize for Literature in 1978, thirty-five years after the destruction of its subject and its audience.

CHAPTER 2

The Short Way to Redemption:
Satan in Goray

In the footsteps of the Messiah [i.e., in the period of his arrival] presumption will increase and respect disappear. The empire will turn to heresy and there will be no moral reproof. The house of assembly will become a brothel, Galilee will be laid waste, and the people of the frontiers will wander from city to city and none will pity them. The wisdom of the scribes will become odious and those who shun sin will be despised; truth will nowhere be found. Boys will shame old men and old men will show deference to boys. "The son reviles the father, the daughter rises up against the mother . . . a man's enemies are the men of his own house" (Micah 7:6). The face of the generation is like the face of a dog. On whom shall we then rely? On our Father in heaven.

—End of the Mishnah Tractate Sota

May he come, but I do not want to see him.

—Sanhedrin 98a

BOTH of the above reactions to the catastrophic character of Messianic redemption as pictured in Jewish sources are to be found in what Gershom Scholem refers to as the most "sober" of Jewish books, the Mishnah and the Talmud. They represent the enormous distance by which the two poles of Jewish sensibility can be separated when contemplating the prospect of the "birth-pangs" of the Messiah, the upheavals believed to be prerequisite to the deliverance of the Jewish people and of humanity. If we keep this fact in mind, we can avoid the temptation to see *Satan in Goray* as merely an exploration of the heterodox, the peripheral, and the bizarre elements in Jewish historical experience. Instead, we can recognize it as an attempt to reconstruct, through the imaginative

22

sympathy of the novelist, one crucial episode in the recurring conflict between tradition and mysticism in the Jewish religion, and
between patience and desperation in a suffering people.

If it were not for the fact that *Satan in Goray* was composed in
1933, we might be tempted to describe the opening scenes of the
novel as a Holocaust setting. The time is 1648, in the immediate
aftermath of the widespread and horrible massacres perpetrated
upon the Jews of Poland by the Ukrainian peasant revolutionary,
Bogdan Chmielnicki. He and his followers, whose enormities per-
meate Singer's historical imagination and are reenacted in many of
his writings, "slaughtered on every hand, flayed men alive, murdered small children, violated women and afterward ripped open
their bellies and sewed cats inside." Europe had never known a
massacre so vast in scale or geographical range. A large proportion
of the Jewish population was murdered, the remainder baptized,
sold into slavery, or—and this is the condition of the characters we
meet in Goray—left amidst the ruins of their existence to ponder
the question of why God's Chosen People have been abandoned to
the bestiality of their uncovenanted oppressors.

Rabbi Benish, the religious leader of the Goray community, offers
the traditional Jewish reply to this question. "To Rabbi Benish the
misfortunes of the years 1648 and 1649 were a punishment visited
on Polish Jews because they had been unfaithful to the Law
. . ."(25). For him the natural response to this latest in the long
series of disasters that compose Jewish history is to rebuild the
community as it was, but presumably with greater and stricter adherence to the Law: " 'Enough! . . . It is the will of our blessed
God that we begin anew' "(6). He thanks God for having left a saving
remnant of the Jewish people in Goray, a narrow margin between
disaster and total destruction.

Without insisting upon the fact, Singer is here commenting upon
the miracle of Jewish survival itself. We know that the Jewish people, very much like other ancient peoples in the Near East, was
subject to expulsion from its homeland, to dispersion, and to per-
secution. But whereas the other ancient peoples who had worshiped
a national god so long as they were in their own land, interpreted
their expulsion and apparent abandonment by God as a sign that
the god was impotent, the Jews always took it for granted that *their*
expulsion and *their* punishments had been inflicted upon them by
God himself for their infidelity to him and to his Law. St. Jerome,

when he beheld the poor Jews in tatters who came to Jerusalem once a year to weep at the remaining wall of their destroyed temple, was sure that he saw the visible sign of God's abandonment of his formerly preferred people; for him the verdict of history was the verdict of God. But the Jews, in defiance of Christian theology, in defiance of history, perhaps in defiance of reason, continued to exist as a people whose loyalty would one day be vindicated by their deliverance.

But not all the Jews of Poland share Rabbi Benish's view that the way to demonstrate continued loyalty to the Jewish God is to rebuild the Jewish community. On the contrary, reports reach Goray to the effect that in Volhynia, the Jews were not rebuilding at all but "had stopped buying houses and sewing heavy overcoats, since it would be warm in the Land of Israel"(39). These Jews have been influenced by the argument that the recent massacres, the most terrible ever inflicted upon the Jewish people, are in fact the birth-pangs of the Messiah, which according to one interpretation of the Kabbalistic text, the Zohar (Book of Splendor), were to start in 1648. If they are indeed to find themselves, in the words of the ancient prayer, "next year in Jerusalem," they will need neither their Polish houses nor (according to the prevailing, and inaccurate, ideas about Jerusalem's climate) warm clothing.

The immediate spur to all this Messianic expectation and speculation is "one great and holy man, Sabbatai Zevi, who was said to be the one for whom Israel had been waiting these seventeen hundred years and who would be revealed in a short time"(22). The historical Sabbatai Zevi was something a good deal less than a "great and holy man," although there is no doubt that his personality hypnotized many truly great and holy men. He was fully educated in the rabbinical tradition, conversant with the Talmudic tradition and also with Kabbalah. What made him unique as a person was a trait which certainly ought not, from the point of view of traditional Judaism, to have strengthened his claim to Messiahship: namely, that in his moments of religious exaltation he was impelled toward spectacular and bizarre violations of the moral law. Since the "holy sinner" was by no means a revered type in Judaism's Messianic tradition, Sabbatai Zevi failed, during the first nineteen years of his sordid career, to gain a single adherent who believed him to be the Messiah. As his biographer has written: "He was laughed at, declared insane, or pitied. No one cared about him until under es-

pecially peculiar circumstances he found a young rabbi of the
Talmud schools in Jerusalem who had settled in Gaza."[1] Nathan of
Gaza, a man of greater intellect and imaginative power than Sabbatai
Zevi, announced in 1665, on the basis of a vision he had received,
that this man who for nineteen years had been regarded by the
Jewish world (and often by himself, too) as a charlatan, was in fact
the Messiah.

Largely as a result of Nathan's propaganda activities as the prophet
of the Messiah, the Sabbatian movement in a short time overwhelmed whole Jewish communities, separated as widely, geo-
graphically and spiritually, as Yemen and England. It was Nathan
who brought enormous numbers of Jews, stricken by grief, to the
inward, emotional experience of redemption, which they then
hoped to see validated in the historical realm by Sabbatai Zevi. But
the historical verdict, as so often in Jewish history, did not vindicate
Jewish hopefulness: "After one year came the catastrophe: in Sep-
tember 1666 Sabbatai Zevi was brought before the Sultan in Ad-
rianople and given the choice of upholding his Messianic claims and
suffering martyrdom, or of converting to Islam. He preferred apostasy from Judaism, which for him in some strange manner seemed
to confirm the paradoxical claim of his Messianic mission, a final
step of holy sinfulness, in fact, its apotheosis."[2]

Singer's depiction of the Sabbatian movement is less fantastic
than the reality. In *Satan in Goray*, the triumph of Sabbatianism
is depicted as a slow process beginning at the time of Sabbatai Zevi's
first appearance in 1648 and culminating in the crisis brought about
for his followers by his conversion to Islam in 1666. Also, the tawdry
character of Sabbatai Zevi himself is barely mentioned in the novel.
Rather, Singer seeks to fathom the inner compulsions which led
large numbers of an ancient people with much experience of false
Messiahs to attach their hopes to so unlikely and unworthy a candidate for Messiahship. As so often in Jewish history, the historical
reality here exceeds any fantasy, and the writer's task is to imagine,
by an act of sympathetic identification, reality itself.

The Jews of Goray are ripe for Messianism not only because they
seek to understand their recent sufferings in relation to God's
scheme for their salvation, but because traditional Judaism seems
inadequate to their needs. Although Singer does not invite any
objection to Rabbi Benish's traditionalism or to his rationalistic opposition to the "contradictory and lewd"(24) cabalistic works of Isaac

Luria, he does make it clear that traditionalism is at this juncture incapable of uniting the household of Israel. The most obvious sign of this inadequacy is Rabbi Benish's failure to unite even his own household, which is a little hell of hatred and discord, father against son, brother against brother; rebbitsin against daughter-in-law. ". . . Rabbi Benish's household was engaged in an interminable family quarrel that had been smoldering for years, since before 1648"(14). The rabbi is himself beset by doubt as a result of the recent slaughter, a doubt which isolates and paralyzes him, even in his duties as a husband: "Rabbi Benish sat alone, locked in, and no longer visited his wife Friday nights in her bedroom"(17).

Now it may well be that traditional Judaism and the traditional community, for all their shortcomings, represent a condition which for the Jews is normal and healthy. It often is the case in Singer's novels that the traditional community, dreary as it looks at first, turns out to be, at the last, far more nourishing to its members than the various exciting alternatives to it. The problem is that the healthy know not of their health; only the sick do. One must break with the traditional community in order to return to it and recognize its sustaining power.

The moribund community of Goray, sleepy and isolated, is stirred into a hideous kind of life, but life nevertheless, by the arrival of a rabbinical legate from Yemen bringing information of Sabbatai Zevi's imminent ascendancy. A local Kabbalist named Mordecai Joseph, both lame and fierce, "a faster, a weeper, an angry man"(42), receives a mystical visitation from Sabbatai Zevi and becomes the first Goray prophet of the coming redemption. His zeal soon brings him into open and violent conflict with Rabbi Benish, whom he has long hated and envied for his learning and fame. Both parties observe the traditional niceties of theological conflict, Benish banning study of the Kabbalah, and Mordecai Joseph administering a murderous beating to a young student of Benish's who suggests that Sabbatai Zevi is in fact a false Messiah.

At this point Singer introduces into the story its only prominent female character, the mysterious and eternally victimized Rechele. She was born in 1648, a few weeks before Chmielnicki's great massacre, and when her mother died five years later was left in the home of her uncle, the ritual slaughterer Zeydel Ber. Rechele lives in terror of this man for the good reason that she observes him at work, and is daily witness to horrifying scenes of animal slaughter, scenes which will recur throughout Singer's fiction. (They will recur in this novel, too, because Rechele's second husband, the satanic Sabbatian prophet Gedaliya, will also be a ritual slaughterer by profession.) She lives in terror of an ancient "Granny" as well, Zeydel's mother-in-law, who beats and persecutes the child, violating her in body and soul in a variety of ways. Even when the granny is dead, Rechele's extraordinary susceptibility to supernatural invasion is foreshadowed by a visitation she receives in her sleep from the dead woman. Her clothes in tatters, her head covered by a blood-soaked kerchief, the dead granny paralyzes Rechele's body with terror, so that for a long time afterwards she is incapable of speech. "Thereafter Rechele was one apart"(68). She regains her speech but has been permanently damaged by this first of many invasions of her soul and her body by supernal powers.

Poor Rechele fears that she has been made into an object of loathing for men, "unless Satan will have me!"(76). Her apparent salvation arrives in Goray in the form of Itche Mates, who is outwardly a packman but in truth devoted entirely to hastening the apotheosis of Sabbatai Zevi, in whose Messiahship he is a faithful believer. Itche Mates offers the book's first exposition of the Sabbatian doctrine. According to it, only a few of the precious divine sparks, which fell with Adam's sin into the realm of impurity, remain in the world, but these are jealously guarded over by the powers of darkness, whose hold is strongest among the Gentiles. These dark forces know that their own existence depends upon continued possession of the divine sparks. Sabbatai Zevi struggles to wrest these divine sparks from the dark powers and return them to their primal, divine origin. An additional element of the Sabbatian doctrine, one not stressed by Itche Mates but by his successor, whom we will meet later, is that the Messiah may be obliged, in order to rescue the divine sparks, to descend in his own person into the depths of impurity where the sparks are imprisoned.[3]

According to Itche's version of Sabbatian doctrine, the triumph of this Messiah would obliterate the need for ritual, for the Talmud, and for all of the Bible except its "essence." Existence would become entirely spiritualized, and the messy business of eating, drinking, and copulating would be done away with; life would be perpetuated through "combinations of holy letters"(73). But since this consum-

mation of earthly existence has yet to be achieved, Itche finds himself physically attracted to the immodest and witchlike Rechele,
even though there is also an element of self-mortification in his
devotion to a woman who is clearly in the grip of supernatural
powers.

Otherwise, Itche's self-mortifications are of a more traditional
ascetic kind. He lacerates himself with thorns and thistles, fasts
"from Sabbath to Sabbath," rolls in snow, and immerses himself in
icy water at the slightest provocation. Perhaps in consequence of
this regimen, or perhaps because he confuses the spiritual realm
toward which his Messianic urge aspires with the material realm
in which he still lives, he finds himself unable to consummate his
marriage with Rechele (whose fear of his "dead eyes"(83) may be
a factor contributing to the fiasco).

The orthodox opponents of Sabbatianism have their own explanation of Itche's impotency, which they send to Rabbi Benish (whose
own relations with his wife, as we have seen, are not the model of
correctness). Although this letter of condemnation, which takes up
a whole chapter of the novel, is too patently partisan and prejudiced
to be accepted at face value, some of its criticism of Itche is convincing; and it must be remembered that its tone and language of
old-fashioned piety, although in striking contrast with the objective
narrative that has thus far characterized the book, are very like the
tone and language of the narrator who takes over from Singer in
the last two chapters of the novel to pass judgment on the action.
The letter's charge of hypocrisy against Itche is not supported by
anything that we know about him; Singer never seems to call his
sincerity into question. But the letter also informs Rabbi Benish
that Itche has married women in town after town only to humiliate
them by his impotence; and this letter arrives long before Itche and
Rechele are married and discover their "incompatibility." The letter
charges that "this false prophet is forever sunk in melancholy, whose
root is lust. . . . From too much magic working, he has himself been
caught in the web, and no longer has the strength to act the man's
part. . ."(91).

Yet in spite of Rabbi Benish's warnings against those who "try to
hasten the end of days" by foolish ascetic zeal, the wedding takes
place amidst a general enthusiasm—from which only the reluctant
Rechele exempts herself—for a marriage which seems to symbolize
the wedding of Sabbatai Zevi with the Jewish people:

Protect, Lord God, this bride and groom;
May we see the Messiah soon.
The Holy Presence, Lord God, wed
As these two seek the marriage bed.

(100)

The high points of the wedding feast are Itche's passionate discourse
on "the mystery of holy sexual union" (99) and his frenzied dance
of mystic enthusiasm with not his bride but a woman named Chin-
kele the Pious. Rabbi Benish is routed, deserted by the community
and, to all appearances, by God as well; and Part One of the novel
ends with his forsaking his congregation and being carted off to
Lublin to die.

Itche Mates, exactly according to the predictions of his conservative rabbinical enemies, and despite the exhortations of his fellow
Sabbatians who urge that "to be fruitful and to multiply is the
principle of principles" (132), proves incapable of consummating his
marriage with Rechele. Whether the failure is due to the fact that
he goes to his bride's bed smelling of "bathhouse water and corpses"
(133) or, as the community believes, to sorcery, Itche is disgraced
and, through his agency, the ascetic interpretation of Sabbatianism
is discredited.

But a successor to Itche Mates is at hand. Wild tales about Sabbatai Zevi's triumphant journey to take the crown of the Sultan (who
then ruled the Land of Israel) are brought to Goray by Reb Gedaliya,
a ritual slaughterer from Zamosc. It is noteworthy that Gedaliya
comes to Goray not only to rally the depressed spirits of the believers in Sabbatai Zevi, but to provide the town with the first ritual
slaughterer it has had since the (human) carnage of 1648. It is as
if the Goray community's readiness to take upon itself the taint of
animal slaughter in order to satisfy its craving for flesh involves it
in a primal sin which brings in its wake all the other sins realized
in the figure of Gedaliya.

Reb Gedaliya hurried about with his green slaughtering knife, expertly
slashing at the shaven necks, and recoiling from the spatter of blood. Butchers moved about with hatches chopping off the heads of the still breathing
beasts, dexterously stripping hides, tearing bodies open, and dragging out
red satin lungs, half-empty stomachs, and intestines. . . . Reb Gedaliya
stood in the center of the slaughterhouse, his knife clenched between his
teeth, his earlocks and his long beard disheveled, his black eyes . . . rolling

as he urged the butchers to finish the examination, remonstrating: "Hurry!
It's clean! It's clean!" (172)

It is his ability to preside over such scenes that makes Gedaliya
acceptable even to the conservative Goray opponents of Sabbatai
Zevi, who because they craved "a spoonful of broth and a bit of
meat, . . .pretended neither to see nor hear" (143).
The Sabbatians themselves are delighted to transfer their alle-
giance from the melancholy and impotent Itche Mates to the exu-
berant and fleshly Gedaliya. His innumerable talents make him the
spiritual leader of the entire Goray community. He can heal bodies,
save souls, offer rabbinical wisdom in the unraveling of abstruse
halachic problems, and charm the rich into giving to the poor more
abundantly than they had ever done. But the prime reason for his
popularity is that he preaches daily, through his "fleshy lips," the
imminent abrogation of all the prohibitions in the Torah and the
Shulchan Aruch, and the universalization of sexual union as the sole
life principle. Whereas Itche Mates envisioned the end of days as
ushering in an era of total spiritualization, Gedaliya argues that the
Messianic era will not merely nullify all the "Thou shalt nots" per-
taining to sexual intercourse, but will in fact require promiscuity
as a religious duty, that is, the inversion of the commandments
which obtained only in the unredeemed world.
Rechele, whose unhappy gift it is to bear upon her flesh the
consequences of every lurch made by her unredeemed community
in the direction of what appears to be redemption, now finds herself
supernaturally impelled into the bed of Reb Gedaliya. Apparently
as a direct result of this union, the angel Sandalfon speaks through
the lips of Rechele the prophecy that the New Year will bring the
Messiah to the Jewish people and the Jewish people to Jerusalem.
Gedaliya, naturally, welcomes this prophetic confirmation of his
own mission, encourages the people to revere Rechele "as though
she were the sacred Torah," and conveniently selects her husband
Itche to go abroad with Mordecai Joseph to spread the news.
The more the people of Goray accept Gedaliya's argument that
redemption requires behavior diametrically opposed to what was
formerly considered Jewish, the more they discard first the external
signs of Jewishness, then the moral law itself. Men and women
discard their head-coverings and dance together in the study-house;
instead of ten men, ten women are called to make a prayer quorum;

women act as cantors and are also called to the lectern on the Sabbath to read from the Torah. The people who were so eager to receive in their midst the man who had the ritual capacity to enable them to eat meat now discover that in fact he has ignored the laws of *kashruth*. Most shocking to the conservative is the rumor, which is later proven correct, that Gedaliya and his acolytes, convinced that Sabbatai Zevi's apotheosis has annulled the old prohibitions, practice adultery and wife-trading and perversions of every kind.

Nothing is so vividly portrayed in *Satan in Goray* as the way in which a community, convinced of the imminence of its redemption, loses all sense of the organic relationship between the Jewish way of life traditionally prescribed for the very reason that it could bring the Jews to redemption, and redemption itself. Abandoning all sense that life is sanctified precisely through the reverence accorded to quotidian existence, the people of Goray suspend all the normal functions of existence because Gedaliya has persuaded them that they are about to be spirited off to Jerusalem.

As the month of Elul approached, the faith of the people of Goray grew stronger. Shopkeepers no longer kept shop, artisans suspended their labors. It seemed useless to complete anything. . . . By winter they would be settled in Jerusalem. And so they tore down fences and outhouses for kindling. Some even ripped the shingles from their roofs. Many refused to undress when they retired at night. (174–75)

Having lost all sense of the distinction between the weekdays and the Sabbath, they have worn out all their Sabbath clothing and so cannot even dress decently for the holiday.

The fact that the failure of the miracle to occur causes the people of Goray to lose all sense of the holiday is the severest possible criticism of Messianism. Do the holidays and the commandments have any intrinsic value, or are they—as Sabbatian Messianism assumes—only a wearisome burden that is to be borne as a punishment while the Jews are in their unredeemed state? Do they lack even the extrinsic value ascribed to them by the belief that only the fullest adherence to them, only that spiritual condition in which the commandments will have been written both upon the doorposts of their houses and upon their hearts, can bring the Messiah? Gedaliya's campaign is the most absolute denial of any relation

between the Torah and the redemption as means and end; the only
relation he posits is one of diametrical opposition, a scheme in which
the Torah is indeed essential, but as one pole of a mad paradox.
Goray has sunk to the state of Sodom and Gomorrah when Mordecai and Joseph return to the town with the shattering news of
Sabbatai Zevi's apostasy to Islam. Gedaliya, already openly accused
of adultery and bloodshed—a frequent combination in Singer—now
finds himself accused of apostasy as well. His reply is that only
Sabbatai Zevi's shadow was converted, but his soul ascended to
heaven. Many former adherents now fall away, and the Sabbatian
loyalists themselves split into two factions. The first believes that
the Messiah will not come until the generation has become completely virtuous; the second believes that the present generation
must become completely guilty before the Messiah can be revealed.

We must recognize that here again Singer is dealing with a historical reality that is more fantastic than what most novelists present
as fantasy. Why should considerable sections of the Jewish people
have continued to believe in the Messiahship of Sabbatai Zevi when,
to all appearances, he had ceased to believe in it himself, at least
not to the point where he was willing to stake his life on his belief?
Singer's answer is that their subjective experience of the imminence
of salvation, at a point in Jewish history when the extremity of their
suffering made salvation more plausible than the continuation of
exile, was stronger than their belief in "objective" historical event.
The extraordinary state of mind which he attempts in the novel to
fathom is suggested by the following utterance of a "moderate"
Sabbatian thirty years after Sabbatai's apostasy: "The Holy One,
blessed be He, does not ensnare even the animals of the righteous,
much less the righteous themselves, to say nothing of so terribly
deceiving an entire people. . . . And how is it possible that all of
Israel be deceived unless this be part of some great divine plan?"[4]

The divine plan, according to Gedaliya and his diehard followers,
compelled Sabbatai Zevi to convert to Islam because it was his
mission to enter the Nether Sphere in his own person in order to
draw out from it the sparks of holiness. Had not the prophet Isaiah
written of the Messiah: "And he shall be reckoned with the sinners"?
Thus the conviction (which has its basis in rabbinic sources) that the
world could be redeemed by the Son of David only in a generation
which was entirely guilty leads Goray into a total corruption, ra-
tionalized by the argument that the Torah of the Messianic era must

be exactly comprised of violations of the Torah of the unredeemed era. This pseudoreligious devotion to anti-Torah is symbolized by Gedaliya's marriage to Rechele, who has not even been divorced from her first husband. That so much of the effort to bring about spiritual purification through total corruption should take the form of wife-trading and other scandalous sexual behavior is a damning comment not only on Sabbatianism but upon the efficacy of the Jewish tradition itself, which after thousands of years does not seem to have been more than skin-deep in its hold upon many of its adherents.

Of all the inhabitants of the area who are thrown into consternation by the monstrous behavior of the Sabbatians who seek redemption through abomination, none is so outraged as are the Polish peasants. Although they play no role in the main action of the novel, they are a sinister presence throughout it. As so often in Yiddish literature, they are characterized by a silence which is a more potent form of utterance than speech: "The peasants in the villages did not speak their wrath. In silence each day they sharpened their scythes, though there was no crop to harvest, in silence they filed the blades of their axes" (171). What kindles their wrath is the abrogation of what they have always taken to be a law of nature: the distinctness of the Jewish people and their religion from all other created things. Although he is writing in 1933, Singer appears already to be urging a truth which will become commonplace in his later, post-Holocaust work: Gentile hostility toward the Jews is not softened but exacerbated by those Jews who seek to become like Gentiles. "In the villages the peasants already complained that the Jews had betrayed their faith and were behaving exactly like gypsies and outlaws. The priests were inciting the masses to a holy war. They foresaw all devout Christians gathering together, sword and spear in hand, to exterminate the Jews, man, woman, and child, so that not a trace should be left of the people of Israel. . ." (202).

The general struggle between the sacred and the profane in Goray is literalized by the battle which takes place for the shattered soul of Rechele, who has been left emptied of piety and the grace of God by the tempestuous events precipitated by Sabbatai Zevi's apostasy. She becomes a theological battleground for the fierce debate between a disembodied face defending the Sacred in a voice and style like that of the forgotten Rabbi Benish, and the audacious, lewd voice of the Profane, regaling her with images of sexual perversion.

As the Profane grows more and more powerful, the path is prepared
for the entry of Satan himself into her body and soul. Reb Gedaliya,
aware that he has been replaced in his bride's bed by Satan himself,
nevertheless pronounces this rape "a goodly vision!" (210). The
victimization of human beings by the irrational forces which prey
upon them if given half a chance is forcefully conveyed by the
Rabelaisian picture of Rechele possessed by Satan:

> At times the evil one blew up one of her breasts. One foot swelled. Her
> neck became stiff. Rechele extracted little stones, hairs, rags, and worms
> from wet, pussy abscesses formed on the flesh of her thigh and under her
> arms. Though she had long since stopped eating, Rechele vomited fre-
> quently, venting reptiles that slithered out tail first. (216)

With the possession of Rechele, Sabbatian zeal abates considerably, and in place of the intellectual and moral frenzy which followed
immediately upon news of the apostasy, resignation and torpor prevail. "There was no longer even sinning; the Evil Spirit himself
seemed to have dozed off. . ." (212–13). Goray is visited by every
conceivable misfortune, natural and supernatural; and Gedaliya,
whose missionary fervor caused all this misery, takes shelter from
the mockery and bitterness of his old followers behind the bolted
shutters of his house.

Thus ends the narrative proper. The teller of this extraordinary
tale has been relatively detached and impartial, as well as entirely
credulous. Demonic visitations are reported in the same objective
manner as are events which, however astonishing in themselves,
do no violence to the natural order of things. The historical episode
of Sabbatai Zevi's brief reign as the Messianic hope of the Jewish
people would seem to carry within it its own moral, since it wrought
in Jewish communities the world over the same havoc which is
described in Goray. Nevertheless, Singer decides to complement
this objective narrative of Satan's rise to power in Goray with a brief
résumé of the whole story by a highly partial, old-fashioned, and
didactic storyteller. Thus the last two chapters of *Satan in Goray*
purport to be excerpts from a work of piety entitled *The Works of
the Earth* which has been translated into Yiddish for the purpose
of giving moral instruction to women, girls, and common folk.

This second narrative differs from the earlier one in that it is not
detached or objective, but passes severe judgment on Gedaliya and

his fellow culprits. It is told in such a way that it seems to have been written at a time much farther removed from the actual events than was the first narrative: "And It Came to Pass in the town of Goray. . ." (220). From this distance the narrator derives not greater perspective but a more absolute moral judgment. We get from his narrative, which takes us back once again to the very beginnings of the story, no indication of the complication of motive on both sides of the conflict, and really no explanation of just how it was that whole communities became ensnared by the ravings of Sabbatai Zevi and his followers. Of the events which made Goray ready to listen to the Sabbatian message, of the fact that the first bearer of the message is not the lascivious Gedaliya but the ascetic Itche Mates; of Rabbi Benish's inadequacies; of all these we hear nothing.

Whereas the first narrative shows us mainly villains and victims, here we have also a hero. He is none other than Mordecai Joseph, the most violent and intolerant of the Goray Sabbatians from the movement's inception there. This pious narrative does indeed mention his earlier descent into Sheol, but now applauds him both for his penitence and for the zeal (not unlike his old Sabbatian zeal) which leads him to smite Gedaliya with a club. We have already received a less favorable picture of the reformed Mordecai in the closing pages of the main narrative, where he is shown agitating against and vilifying all of the faithful except Rechele.

What makes Mordecai Joseph the hero of the novel's brief closing narrative, however, is his act of exorcising from the tormented body of Rechele the dybbuk which has possessed it. The plight of Rechele moves even this pious narrator to the most lurid detail, which pictures a woman with legs permanently spread because it is through *"that same place"* (227) that the dybbuk entered her. This dybbuk, a native of Lublin who had devoted his youth to defilement of the Sabbath, to sexual perversions, and to obsessively repeating—the first of many characters in Singer novels to do so—"There is neither Justice nor Judge" (224), offers to strike a bargain with Mordecai Joseph and his other besiegers. Rechele, he maintains, has only regained her health and remained alive because of his agency; if he is allowed to remain inside her, he will protect her and keep her strong. But Mordecai refuses the offer and proceeds to exorcise the dybbuk. Once he is exorcised, the conclusions toward which the main narrative seemed to be pointing are swiftly realized: Rechele at once, just as the dybbuk had predicted, loses her strength and dies;[5] Itche, her penitent first husband, dutifully follows her into death; and Gedaliya becomes an apostate and a persecutor of the Jews.

This short concluding narrative is both a contrast and a complement to what has preceded it. On the one hand, Singer wants to show the different aspects under which Sabbatianism appears to the dispassionate historical novelist and to the Jewish moralist. The first narrator, the novelist, wants to understand the complex motivation which led the Jewish people to seek the consummation of their long historical experience through the agency of a false Messiah; the moralist is less interested in the experiential reality of the historical situation than in its moral implications for the Jewish people. The didactic and hortatory tone of the last two chapters and the fact that they have been translated into Yiddish to satisfy the moral needs of those members of the community who cannot read the sacred tongue identify them with an older kind of Yiddish literature from which Singer certainly wanted to dissociate himself. Yet it is noteworthy that the first narrator is not allowed to complete the story; this must be done from the wider, though more simplified, perspective of the pious narrator.

Nor is the essential correctness of the moralist's judgment upon the events of the novel called into question. It should be remembered that in the narrative proper there was, for the brief length of one chapter, the eleventh, also a substitute narrator in the person of the Lublin rabbi who, in a language also redolent of didactic piety, warned against Itche and Sabbatianism. Simpleminded as his letter sounded in relation to the novel's characteristic tone of sophisticated detachment, its predictions proved correct in every particular. This fact may put us in mind of Singer's remark, quoted in Chapter 1, that his father was, "from his point of view," right to say that "secular writers like Peretz were leading the Jews to heresy."[6] Singer may himself be committed to a novelistic interpretation of historical events, but he is still willing to give the last word of his novel to the religious moralist.

This last word is explicit in its condemnation of all those who are no longer content to await the coming of the ever-tarrying Messiah, but seek through action to hasten his arrival:

LET NONE ATTEMPT TO FORCE THE LORD: TO END OUR PAIN WITHIN THE WORLD: THE MESSIAH WILL COME IN GOD'S OWN TIME. . . . (239)

Singer's later experience of secularized versions of Messianism
would lead him to endorse more categorically this condemnation
of forcing the end of a bad situation by making it still worse. Yet
he knows, and demonstrates in this novel, that two things deeply
embedded in Jewish experience lend plausibility to each new promise of an historical end in a time of unspeakable suffering. One is
the inescapable, if unfortunate, fact that, to cite Gershom Scholem
once more, "Jewish Messianism is in its origins and by its nature
. . . a theory of catastrophe" which stresses the inevitability of a
cataclysm in the transition from historical present to Messianic future.[7] The other is the inability of the Jewish people to explain to
themselves what seems to be a cosmic conspiracy to make them
suffer without resorting to the belief that redemption is at hand.
Singer asks us to put ourselves into the position of people who ask
themselves, in the wake of suffering such as no other people has
endured: "Is it possible that after all this nothing is expected of us
but to return to the old routines? Is it not rather the case that no
generation is likely to come as close as our own to being completely
evil, and that rather than try to return the world to 'business as
usual' we should do all that we can to bring this evil generation to
its logical consummation?"
Anyone who doubts the plausibility of this train of thought to a
truly religious mind in the mid-twentieth century need only look
at one of the best-known diaries written by a Jewish victim of the
German process of destruction, that of young Moshe Flinker. This
sixteen-year-old Dutch Jew, a young man of great intelligence and
acute moral sensibility, expresses throughout the diary which he
kept in 1942–43 a passionate desire for redemption. He wants Messianic redemption not only because it will end the sufferings of the
Jewish people, but because it will prove that these sufferings had
a meaning. It is for this reason that he wants not the English, but
the Germans—of whose monstrous deeds he is well informed—to
win the war. "The prophet foretold that we would not return to
[Eretz Israel] because of our righteousness but as a result of the
evildoing of our enemies and our agony at their hand. . . ." For
young Moshe the war and the destruction of the Jews mark the end
of the exile and the birth-pang of the Messiah. Should the Germans
be beaten, what then? At best (not that Moshe ever expects this
best) the Jews would return to their former state of exile, and all
that had happened would have been "for nothing."[8]
In his later novels of modern life Singer will frequently deal with

the Jewish Messianic longing and its perversions, but these will generally be political in character, and in *The Slave* he will return to the situation of the Jews in the aftermath of the Chmielnicki massacre. There is, however, at least one later work which offers a sort of gloss on the subject of *Satan in Goray*. It is the short story entitled "The Destruction of Kreshev,"which was originally published in the same volume that contained the 1943 reissue of *Satan in Goray* in Yiddish and may be found in *The Spinoza of Market Street*. Unlike *The Slave*, which is also set in Poland in the immediate aftermath of the Chmielnicki massacres, it takes place at a time when Sabbatai Zevi "the False Messiah was long dead" (188), yet its concerns are those of *Satan in Goray*. This story (to be more fully discussed in Chapter 9) shares both the distant perspective and the severity of judgment which characterized the coda to *Satan in Goray*, but whereas the novel's conclusion expressed the viewpoint of the pious, "Destruction of Kreshev" is entirely narrated by Satan himself, and there is never any question but that Sabbatianism is the devil's work.

Why did the same Singer who in 1933 had presented Sabbatianism not as unmitigated charlatanry and evil but as a resort by large numbers of the Jewish people to an apocalyptic explanation and resolution of their suffering, in 1943 present it as devil's work precipitating—in the words of the central villain of "Destruction of Kreshev"—a "holocaust"? The answer may lie in the fact that by 1943 the "final" holocaust of the Jewish people in Europe was under way; the extent to which false Messianism of every kind was responsible for this unprecedented destruction was to be the subject of Singer's next novel.

CHAPTER 3

The Family Moskat

Israel is desolated; its seed is no more.

—Merneptah, King of Egypt, 1215 B.C.E.

L IKE most of the great modern novels which record the history
of a family, *The Family Moskat* describes a process of disintegration whereby the unity of the family is shattered by a variety of
assertions of individual will against the dead hand of the past. But
a novel which takes as its subject the life of Polish Jewry from the
early part of the twentieth century until the moment of Hitler's
entry into Warsaw cannot, if its author is a man of moral sensitivity,
end its story with a picture of emancipated individuals pursuing
their separate destinies. For the Jewish people of Europe, and the
Moskat family of Singer's novel, found themselves, at the very
moment of their greatest internal disintegration and disunity, in-
tegrated and united by a common destiny: the violent death that
was to be dealt by the Germans to every Jew of Europe. The striking
paradox of modern Jewish history, whereby people were to be reminded horribly of their common destiny at the very moment when
they had virtually forgotten their shared history, provides Singer
with the principle that unifies his vision of the phantasmagoria that
was Jewish life in Poland in the twentieth century. For each of the
myriad characters in the novel, therefore, Singer must weave two
stories simultaneously. On the one hand we follow the stories of
individuals who are ruled by passion or love or politics or ideology
or religion; on the other we see their stories as only infinitely varied
repetitions of the single story of the Jewish people thrown into the
storm-center of modern history by antisemitism and two world wars.

Although we and Singer recognize these two kinds of story to be
inseparable from each other, characters in the novel (unless they

39

happen to be Zionists) generally do not. Often the moment of revelation about a character, to himself or to others, will consist of the
recognition that the two stories intersect. Thus Hadassah Moskat,
one of the family patriarch's many errant grandchildren, is from her
youth attracted to Christianity, and her disappointments in worldly
life make her envy Christian girls, who can enter a convent. "If she
was opposed to apostasy, it was for one reason only: it was the Jews
who were the persecuted, not the Christians. If what the Evangelist
said was true, that the meek would inherit the earth, then the Jews
were the real Christians" (420). Her cousin Masha does convert to
Catholicism in order to wed the Judeophile Polish painter Yanek;
but Yanek, like so many of his countrymen who eagerly anticipated
the arrival of Hitler, becomes an antisemite and finds a victim ready
to hand in his wife, who for him is still a Jew. Asa Heshel Bannet,
the proverbial "young man—from the provinces," is a scion of the
root of King David. But he comes to Warsaw to emulate Spinoza
by seeking enlightenment and happiness through secular learning.
Shortly after arrival he discards his Chassidic garments and is wel-
comed by the enlightened friends who congratulate him: " 'You
look like a *goy* ' " (144). But a few hours later he enters a restaurant
whose owner tells him to " 'go back to Palestine' " (147). When
Adele Landau first comes to Warsaw, she justifies Polish antisemitism by saying that these backward, "Asiatic" Jews have brought
China into Poland. But a quarter-century later, when Polish antisemitism forces her to flee to Palestine, and British cynicism sends
her back to Poland (and to Hitler), no one needs to tell her that the
problem is not one of manners but of Jewish identity.

The traditional community is a wide-branching tree whose roots
cannot be fathomed by the conscious mind. This is true both literally
and figuratively. Singer provides us with meaning as well as useful
information by giving, at the beginning of the novel, diagrams of
the family trees of the Moskat family itself, the Bannet and Katzenellenbogen families, and even the family of Koppel Berman, the
parvenu who enters the Moskat family by criminal means. Within
the story itself, we are told that Asa Heshel's maternal grandfather,
Reb Dan Katzenellenbogen, "had a genealogical chart of his own,
inscribed on parchment with gold ink in the form of a many-
branched linden tree. The root was King David, and the branches
bore the names of other illustrious forebears" (25). When Asa returns with his wife, Adele, for his first visit to his family in the

village of Tereshpol Minor after having seen and experienced much of the non-Jewish world, he is met on the road by a natural symbol of what is uprooted when Jewish traditional culture is destroyed: "It was lined with great trees, chestnut and oak. Some of them had huge gashes torn in their sides by bolts of lightning. The holes looked dark and mysterious, like the caves of robbers. Some of the older trees inclined their tops down toward the ground, as though they were ready to tumble over, tearing up with them the tangled thickness of their centuries-old roots" (240).

Having said this, we must also recognize that the privilege of seeing a traditional culture as mysterious and sacred in its organic unity generally belongs to a spectator with the wisdom of hindsight rather than to a living participant in the culture. The young Moskats and their spouses are more likely to see traditional Jewish culture as being uprooted precisely because the topmost branches of the older trees incline towards the ground instead of aspiring to the heavens. The early sections of the novel depict, in the Moskat family and also in Asa Heshel Bannet and any number of others, the mass defection of young people from Judaism and, to a lesser extent, from the Jewish people, both of which are for them embodied in their elders.

The story opens with the third marriage of Reb Meshulam Moskat, the wealthy patriarch of the Moskat family. No sooner has he formalized the marriage to the widow Rosa Frumetl Landau than he regrets it, for the very good reason that "The masculine ripple that had awakened in him during his courtship soon flickered and died. In their bedchamber his bride revealed herself to be a broken shell." Several of Moskat's seven children and more of his grandchildren will inherit his susceptibility to sexual passion, but few will show his determination to accept the responsibility for such indulgences. Although tempted to dissolve the marriage promptly, he finally decides "to follow the wisdom of the sages—the best thing to do is to do nothing" (19). He returns with his new wife—who brings with her not only an irritating "European" daughter, Adele, but also a formidable unpublished manuscript by her late husband— to Warsaw, to his vast business holdings, and to a family of very grown-up and very dependent children, who support themselves by acting as administrators of his various properties. In fact, the only one besides the old man who knows anything of the management of the business is Koppel the bailiff, who acts as Meshulam's

adviser and confidant. Cut very much according to the model of
Uriah Heep, Koppel stresses his meekness and his subservience to
his superior at every opportunity.

Reb Meshulam Moskat, though not an intensely religious man,
and at odds with the leaders of Warsaw's Jewish community, is a
loyal follower of the Chasidic rabbi of Bialodrevna, to whose court
he makes regular pilgrimage. The rabbi of Bialodrevna, whose own
daughter Gina Genendel has disgraced him by leaving her husband
and frequenting the Warsaw society of "heretics and mockers," is
the book's first general critic of modern tendencies which are shattering the community of Israel.

But what of Israel, what of the people Israel! Heresy was growing day by
day. In America—so he had heard it said—Jews violated the Sabbath. In
Russia, in England, in France, Jewish children were growing up in ignorance of Holy Writ. And here in Poland, Satan roamed openly through the
streets. Youths were running away from the study houses, shaving off their
beards, eating the unclean food of the gentile. Jewish daughters went about
with their naked arms showing, flocked to the theaters, carried on love
affairs. Never had it been so bad as this, even in the times of Sabbathai
Zevi and Jacob Frank, may the names of the false messiahs be blotted out
for eternity. Unless the cursed plague were halted, not a remnant would
be left of Israel. What was He waiting for, the almighty God? Did He want
to bring the Redeemer to a generation steeped in sin? (81–82)

The rabbi's description of the disintegration of the Jewish community in the aftermath of the 1905 Revolution is essentially accurate. But neither the Bialodrevna rabbi, nor Asa Heshel's
grandfather, Rabbi Dan Katzenellenbogen, who is presented, without qualification, as a saint, is prepared to meet the challenge of
modernity. Their Judaism has made itself into a fortress, and like
most fortresses it suffers from stationariness and an inability to take
the offensive. One indication of its intransigence is to be found in
its violent hostility to Zionism, which is viewed as a heretical desire
to build the Jewish homeland without waiting for the Messiah to
come. Something, though by no means all, of Singer's attitude to
the Orthodox condemnation of modernity *in toto* may be seen from
the fact that the Bialodrevna faithful place the blame for all that has
happened to their young on "these worldly books, printed in Yiddish
so that anyone could understand. . ." (165–66).

Primary among the enemies which threaten the existence of the community of Israel is romantic love. Its attractions, and its ultimate inadequacy, are illustrated through a large number of characters in the novel, but primarily through the one love affair whose career is almost coextensive with the entire novel, that between Asa Heshel Bannet and Hadassah Moskat, the granddaughter of Meshulam. Hadassah, whose mother, Dacha, has educated her in "modern," that is, non-Jewish, schools, refuses the match that has been arranged for her with Fishel Kutner, a devout Chasid and heir to a fortune. Meshulam sees the opposition of his granddaughter (supported by her mother) as a challenge not merely to his authority, but to his life: "In his long career he had overcome more formidable opponents than Dacha and Hadassah. . . . If he were to lose a single [struggle], it would be the signal for his death" (85). The rabbi of Bialodrevna, when told of Hadassah's resistance, concludes: " 'Maybe she's fallen in love—God forbid' " (87). Romantic love, more certainly than other Western importations such as rationalism or socialism or nationalism, signaled the breakup of traditional Jewish society because, in the view of the rabbis, it denied the true purpose of marriage, and epitomized the futile pursuit of happiness apart from religion.

The rabbi of Bialodrevna would hardly have been surprised to learn that the heretical young devotee of Spinoza with whom Hadassah had, in fact, fallen in love, was at work on a manuscript entitled "The Laboratory of Happiness," which developed plans for the "establishment of a research laboratory for experimentation in pure happiness" (493) and advocated "more sex and fewer children" (497) as the key to all social and individual problems. Asa Heshel arrives in Warsaw with the maledictions of his grandfather, his mother's prayer that Elijah will look after him, and a letter of recommendation from the *maskil* (devotee of secular Western knowledge), principal of the modern Jewish school of Zamosc, who hopes his neophyte will enter a university. Asa is introduced into the midst of the Moskat family through the agency of Abram Shapiro, who is married, unhappily, to Meshulam's daughter Hama. Abram, who is a little bit of a Chasid, something of a Zionist, and most of all a lecher, is a character of considerable wisdom, but only in those things which are unrelated to his personal life, which is a disaster. His indiscriminate lust ranges widely, and his own niece Hadassah is among its objects, although he always behaves with complete propriety toward her. It is he who encourages the affair between Asa and

Hadassah, although with misgivings both on his own account and that of the family, especially when the affair becomes sordid and painful. Hadassah and Asa Heshel elope on the eve of her wedding, intending to live in Switzerland. But they are intercepted by soldiers at the border with Austria. Hadassah is arrested and then, after spending time in jail, is returned to her parents more dead than alive. Asa Heshel then marries Adele, who has been in love with him ever since he undertook to edit her father's manuscript, and Hadassah, angry and bitter, follows suit by making a loveless marriage with Fishel Kutner, donning the matron's wig "just as though it were my cross." Hadassah's vaguely Christian aspirations come out most clearly at this crisis in her life, for she blames Judaism for not giving her the solace she requires after the abortive affair with Asa. "Why don't we have the kind of religion where a Jewish girl can go into a synagogue and kneel in prayer before God? . . . Please, Father in heaven, give me back my faith" (210–11).

Hadassah's need for faith makes her, in the eyes of Asa Heshel, the polar opposite to himself, and perhaps for that reason all the more attractive. When they are planning their elopement, he asks himself: " 'How can I aspire to her? She's all belief, I'm all doubt. I'll only do her harm' " (150). Whereas Hadassah believes in God, in mankind, and in romantic love, Asa "had nothing but doubt about everything" (369). In the event, Asa's fears prove justified. Both of them will prove scandalously unfaithful to their spouses, but Hadassah's fidelity to her original love will not be returned by Asa.

Singer's depiction of the love affair between Hadassah and Asa cannot, however, be described merely as an instance of the easy attraction but ultimate incompatibility of faith and doubt, for Singer is too comprehensive an observer of the rich confusion of human relations to allow for schematization of his stories. No sooner has Asa married Adele than he writes to Hadassah telling her that his single goal in life is to be united again with the only woman he has ever loved. Apparently it is his longing for Hadassah that causes him to inflict endless pain upon his wife, Adele, whom he also forces into two abortions—for it is not romance that peoples the Jewish world. Unfortunately for herself, Adele's devotion to Asa is as single-minded as Hadassah's. Thus she explains to her mother that she cannot think of leaving him because "I'm not one of those women who love one man today and another tomorrow. I'm like those insects that can love only once" (225).

Both Adele and Fishel Kutner enter into marriages which they know full well are made with unwilling partners. Adele "had known, the very day she dragged him to the canopy, that he loved Hadassah, not her" (232), and Fishel had the identical proof of Hadassah's primary devotion to Asa. From the romantic point of view, then, the disastrous termination of both these marriages is hardly remarkable. Yet from Singer's point of view what is of primary significance is that the passionate (and adulterous) relationship of Asa and Hadassah, even before it is legitimized by their marriage, turns to ashes in the mouth, whereas the unromantic and unloved Adele and Fishel evince a devotion to their unfaithful spouses which remains a mystery to the objects of their love. Long after Asa has deserted her for Hadassah, Adele directly professes to him her continued love and pleads with him—for he is now involved with yet another woman, Barbara Fishelsohn—not to desert his ailing wife, Hadassah. She is able to do this not because she is an embodiment of selflessness, but because she allows the past to speak through her: "As Adele spoke she had a strange feeling that it was someone else speaking through her lips. It was her dead mother saying these words, her voice and her intonation" (545). Hadassah is still more mystified than Asa by the fact that all the shame and disgrace she has heaped on Fishel have not uprooted his love for her: " 'Why should he still care for me?' " she wondered. " 'Who is he, this man I married? Is this what his study of the Talmud teaches him?' " (351).

This mystery is rooted in the nature of Jewish religion. Not long after Asa has first committed adultery with Hadassah, "the thought suddenly flashed through his mind that there was a profound connection between the fourth and seventh commandments" (277). The injunction to keep the Sabbath is an injunction to sanctify time, whereas the act of adultery desecrates time by abrogating the love that is a function of slow growth in favor of peremptory and whimsical demands of lust. The novel is obsessed by the nature and the effects of time. "Time," says Asa early in the book, "makes refuse of all things" (99). Few books by Singer keep us so fully aware of the Jewish calendar as *The Family Moskat*. Singer knows that determination of the calendar has, ever since the destruction of the

Second Temple, been one of the most important of rabbinical functions. "Judaism," says Abraham Heschel, "teaches us to be attached to *holiness in time,* to be attached to sacred events, to learn how to consecrate sanctuaries that emerge from the magnificent stream of a year. The Sabbaths are our great cathedrals; and our Holy of Holies is a shrine that neither the Romans nor the Germans were able to burn; a shrine that even apostasy cannot easily obliterate: the Day of Atonement."[1]

Nowhere is the essential opposition between romantic love and the community of Israel illustrated more dramatically than in the way Asa and Hadassah become more brazen and perverse in their lust when they indulge it during the Ten Penitential Days and on the Day of Atonement itself.

Having profaned the holiest day she yielded to all his impulses. She gave herself to him on the chair, on the carpet, on Fishel's bed. Asa Heshel dozed off and awoke, frightened by a dream, blazing with passion. Hadassah sighed in her sleep. Asa Heshel got up from the bed and stood at the window. Yes, this was he, Asa Heshel. His father, half insane, had died somewhere in a filthy little hamlet in Galicia. Generations of rabbis, saints, rabbinical wives, had purified themselves in order that he might be born. And here he was spending the night of Yom Kippur with another man's wife! (315–16)

Indeed, as Asa says later in the book, "How strange time is!" People, Singer seems to say in a variety of ways, become human not because they acquire, in their own lifetime, happiness or political rights or emancipation; they become human insofar as they are capable of inheriting the legacy of their ancestors and transmitting this in turn to their descendants. Abram Shapiro, in the midst of a dismal encounter with his ailing mistress Ida, is struck by the way in which even inanimate objects take on meaning because they express the humanity which we inherit from past generations: "He took out the string of pearls that he had got at Hadassah's. He looked carefully at each pearl. How old, he wondered, were they? Dacha had got them from her mother, and her mother had got them from her mother when she was married. Yes, people died, but things lived on" (478).

Although the marriage between Asa and Hadassah is the consummation of love and romance, it too proves a failure. Once married, Asa falls in love with a Communist party functionary, Barbara

Fishelsohn, the daughter of a convert, and Hadassah is left miserable and abandoned with their child, Dacha. Asa has always believed, with Spinoza, that happiness and morality are identical and that "the only goal of humanity was enjoyment" (469). But the hunger for happiness grows by what it feeds on, and is in fact insatiable. The trail of ruined lives which is laid by Asa's intrepid search for happiness proves that what he really craves is not love but irresponsibility. Hadassah explains his inability to sustain permanent relationships or to be responsible other than monetarily to the children he has fathered, as the inevitable outcome of his lack of faith: "He doesn't believe in anything—not God, or humanity. . . . I'm afraid that he doesn't know what love is. He recognizes only physical passion" (427–28). But Adele, who has suffered longer because of Asa's insatiable pursuit of happiness, sees the situation more accurately. At the moment of her very last meeting with him, Adele understands that Asa's endless bitterness and malaise came not from his failure to achieve a career or to find satisfaction in love: ". . . Suddenly she knew: he was not a worldly man by his very essence. He was one of those who must serve God or die. He had forsaken God, and because of this he was dead—a living body with a dead soul. She was astonished that this simple truth had eluded her until now" (582).

There is much in the book to support the generalization that, as Asa himself says at one point, every modern Jew is spiritually ill, and in his desperate search for what cannot be found—happiness without God—injures those around him. At a masquerade ball late in the novel, at which he first meets Barbara, Asa sees all these secularized Jews as "exiled vagabonds" joylessly pursuing joy. "They had lost God and had not won the world" (491). Ironically, some of them put on the masks of their deserted, but better, selves only in play. "Russian generals with epaulets, Polish grandees in elegant caftans, Germans in spiked helmets, rabbis in fur hats, yeshivah students in velvet skullcaps; sidelocks dangling below their ears. It was some time before Hadassah realized that these were merely masquerade costumes" (487).

Although the Asa-Adele-Hadassah triangle is the most relentlessly pursued, it is only the most prominent example of a pattern which is repeated in stories of lesser characters who seek happiness and fulfillment through love. Meshulam Moskat's daughter Leah deserts her unworldly Chasidic husband, Moshe Gabriel, the father of her

four children, for the sensually attractive Koppel Berman, who has
gained his fortune by robbing Leah's father's safe and pauperizing
her brothers and sisters. Even before the divorce takes place, Leah
wonders to herself how she can desert a "saint" like Moshe Gabriel
for a scoundrel like Koppel; and after some years' experience of
Koppel's criminality and philandering she wonders still more. Koppel becomes so accustomed, after his many conquests, to seeing
every woman as his potential partner in bed, that he nearly stumbles
into the primal sin: "Not far from the hotel entrance he saw a girl,
hatless and with a creased jacket much too big for her, in a too long,
old-fashioned skirt. He stood and looked at her. One of those street-
walkers? No, they did not dress like that. Maybe she was a beginner
out for the first time. He crossed the street toward her, strange
thoughts blundering through his mind. . . . Suddenly he froze in
his tracks. There was something familiar about her, though he could
not say exactly what. She was waving to him and running toward
him. It was Shosha. Koppel felt a sudden dryness in his throat.
'What are you doing here?' he stammered. 'Oh, Papa, I've been
waiting for you—' " (462). The crude and selfish Koppel may seem
far removed in spirit from Asa Heshel, but they are united by their
participation in the indiscriminateness of lust: "[Asa's] sleep had
been full of visions—corpses, funerals, reptiles, beasts. There was
rape, slaughter, fire, torture. He was lying with his sister, Dinah,
and with Dacha, his daughter. He even had unclean relations with
his dead mother" (561). Once the marital bonds prescribed by religion are broken, anything is possible.

The novel is pervaded by striking visual images attesting to the
futility and ultimate sadness of those who, in disregard of the wider
interests of the Jewish people, pursue the happiness which love
seems to offer. In the face of Ida Prager, Abram Shapiro's sick and
aging mistress, "the rouge had cracked like whitewash on a wall.
There was a deep sorrow in her look, the despair of one whose life
had become entangled in an error that it was now too late to set
right" (395). Abram Shapiro suffers a heart attack in the bed of
Meshulam's former servant Manya, and suffers a terrible revelation
simultaneously: "Manya . . . drew off her nightgown, standing there
naked, with her pendulous breasts, broad hips, flat belly, hairy legs.
. . . So this was the bargain he had given up his life to possess! It
occurred to him that he ought to pronounce the prayer for forgiveness, but he could not capture the words" (500).

Yet the words do continue to sound, and at times they can transform, albeit temporarily, the lives even of those who have almost forgotten them. The general picture which Singer gives us of Polish Jewry is not an attractive one, and is as far removed as is possible from the images of Hitler's victims which the postwar public has received from Chagall and the Broadway version of Sholom Aleichem. Almost everywhere there is petty bickering, narrow materialism, and spiritual squalor. Despite or because of the frantic pursuit of happiness, Hadassah is correct in saying, " 'No one in the family is really happy' " (156). The Bannet family too seethes with jealous rivalries. Abram wonders: " 'What did they want, these people? Why were they all eager to tear one another to pieces?' " (476). In the midst of this almost unrelieved darkness, only their inherited religion seems capable of giving these Jews some vestige of a human life.

Virtually the only occasions in the novel which are uplifting and joyous are those holidays when Jews are commanded to rejoice. Early in the novel, there is a Chanukah celebration presided over by Meshulam Moskat in his patriarchial robes; here the Moskat family, to which we are introduced, is still intact. A good deal later, we witness the gathering of sons, daughters, in-laws, and grandchildren at Meshulam's house, even though he himself is ill. But Abram, who has quarreled with his father-in-law and his wife, Hama, is forced to make do with a bottle of wine shared with Ida, who lives apart from her husband and child: "The daughter of a pious and well-to-do family, Ida had been used to joyous Purim celebrations. But now she, too, was alone" (195–96). Still later in the novel, on the eve of the first of the German occupations of Warsaw during World War I, the bitterness, loneliness, and joylessness of the Moskats are dissipated by Simchat Torah, the Rejoicing of the Law. On such an occasion, depicted with great beauty by Singer, even so misused a wife as Hama can be filled with joy and love of her husband, who on Simchat Torah seems even to the pious to be " 'one of our own. A Chassid to his bones!' " Her prayer for her husband is also a prayer for all the Jews of this world: " 'If he could only be like this all through the year!' " (309). If only all the Jews could rejoice in the Law and not seek after their own hearts, how different everything could be!

Yet adherence to religion would not have saved the community of Israel in Europe. If religion is a positive, it is as little capable of altering, or even comprehending, the historical fate of the Jewish people, as any other force in the novel. In fact, the religious do not, in the novel, recognize the existence of the Jewish people as an entity separable from Judaism. When Asa Heshel apologetically tells his grandfather Dan Katzenellenbogen that despite his desertion of Chasidism he had attended the celebration for the Rejoicing of the Law in Lausanne, the rabbi asks why Jews whose lives are not coextensive with their religion but only with a few major holidays should remain Jews at all. "If God had lost all meaning for them, and the world was without design, how could they justify calling themselves Jew?" Asa's Zionist argument that the Jews "were a people like every other people" (238) is incomprehensible to the old man.

If many secular characters in the novel pursue their aims in disregard of the historical fate which is enveloping them, the religious seem to deny the very existence of historical forces that are not determined by the Jewish God. The most perceptive of the religious characters, Asa's grandfather, does recognize that evil reigns in the lower world. But, as he surveys the wreckage of his community after the Jews are expelled from Tereshpol Minor at the outbreak of World War I, he resists the idea of a radical evil, of a Satan who is *not* in the employ of God. "He comforted himself with the knowledge that everything came from God. Even the Devil had his roots in the divine creation" (262). At the outbreak of World War II, the Chasidic response to the approach of Hitler and the imminent destruction of the Jewish people is symbolized by Asa Heshel's brother-in-law, Menassah David, who does nothing but dance. "For what, after all, was the great trick in showing ecstasy only in time of plenty? The true greatness was in giving oneself up to joy when the waters were rising around one" (541).

By demonstrating the inadequacy of Jewish religion to the task of comprehending the dimensions of the threat which antisemitism presents to the Jewish people, Singer does not endorse the agnostic or skeptical response to it. Rather he creates a series of parallel scenes meant to show that faith and skepticism alike remain baffled by the mystery and enormity of Jewish suffering. In the aforementioned scene where Rabbi Dan Katzenellenbogen guides the exodus of his people from Tereshpol Minor (to the great joy of their Polish neighbors), he is assailed with the all-expressive "Nu?" by the town

freethinker and apostle of Western enlightenment, Jekuthiel the
watchmaker:

> "*Nu,* rabbi?" he said.
> It was clear that what he meant was: Where is your Lord of the Universe
> now? Where are His miracles? Where is your faith in Torah and prayer?
> "*Nu,* Jekuthiel," the rabbi answered. What he was saying was: Where
> are your worldly remedies? Where is your trust in the gentiles? What have
> you accomplished by aping Esau? (259–60)

To Jekuthiel it seems inescapably clear that the Jewish God has
been far less faithful to His people than they to Him; and to Rabbi
Dan it seems just as clear that if God cannot help the Jews, nothing
can, for what salvation can there be in imitating the ways of the
oppressors? Both are right in what they deny, but unsupported in
what they affirm. In any case, as Rabbi Dan says to himself, "The
old riddle remained: the pure in heart suffered and the wicked
flourished; the people chosen of God were still ground into the
dust. . ." (229).
A similar parallelism is created between Rabbi Dan and his grandson Asa Heshel. Both labor during a lifetime over manuscripts grap-
pling with the ultimate questions. The grandfather had produced
three sackfuls of manuscripts and "there had been a time when he
had entertained the idea of publishing some of his commentaries."
But a few days after the outbreak of World War I, "he crammed
his manuscripts into the mouth of the stove and then watched them
burn. 'The world will survive without them,' he remarked" (258).
Asa Heshel, a few days after the outbreak of World War II, repeats
Jekuthiel's question, asking Barbara, " 'What do you think of God
now, tell me' " (599). But he acknowledges the futility of his own
hedonistic solution: "In the drawer of his desk lay an old version
of 'The Laboratory of Happiness,' written in Switzerland. Asa
Heshel unscrewed the door of the stove and thrust it inside" (605).
If the mystery of Jewish suffering cannot be fathomed by the
intellectual efforts of either the believers or the skeptics, perhaps
the best response to the fact of this suffering would be an existential
one, in which action would cut through the knot that intellect has
been unable to untie. "Get thee out of thy country" is an injunction
with deep roots in Jewish consciousness, and one which sounds in

the ears of several characters in *The Famly Moskat,* including Asa
Heshel himself, who, after his first brush with antisemitism in
Warsaw, says to himself: " 'Yes, Abram is right. I've got to get out
of Poland. If not to Palestine, then to some other country where
there's no law against Jews going to college" (147).

Since Abram Shapiro is the most prominent spokesman for Zionism among the novel's major characters, the book can hardly be
said to be a Zionist tract. Nevertheless, Zionism is clearly set apart
from socialism, communism, and other left-wing movements which
arouse the wrath of the orthodox, for the very good reason that only
Zionism grasped the dimensions of twentieth-century antisemitism
and understood its implication for the future of the Jewish people.
Abram rails against the Jewish intellectuals who gain their university
credentials by loudly proclaiming that Jews are a religion, not a
nation, and that the backward, dirty Jews from the East pollute the
Western European atmosphere. He insists again and again that the
Exile alone has made of the Jews the "cripples, *schlemiels,* lunatics"
(140) who inhabit Warsaw: " 'Just let us be a nation in our own land
and we'll show what we can do. Ah, the geniuses'll tumble out of
their mothers' bellies six at a time—like in Egypt' " (44). Abram's
claims for Zionism are expressed with the extravagance that characterizes all his utterances. Yet he sees with perfect lucidity what
is concealed, by vanity or self-interest or even good will, from the
eyes of the assimilationists, all those characters in the novel who
prefer Polish to Yiddish, who shorten their coats and their hair, and
seek to become indistinguishable from the Gentiles: To Adele, for
example, he acerbically remarks: " 'And I suppose if we all put on
Polish hats and twist our mustaches into points, then they'll love
us,' Abram rejoined, and twisted at his own mustache. 'Let the
young lady read the newspapers here. They squeal that the modern
Jew is worse than the caftaned kind. Who do you think the Jew-
haters are aiming for? The modern Jew, that's who' " (46). All the
subsequent events of the novel are to bear out what Abram says.

Apart from the Orthodox, the most active opponents of Zionism
in the novel are the Socialist and Communist revolutionaries whose
devotion to "humanity" slackens only in relation to the Jews. *The
Family Moskat* is the first major work by Singer in which the intensity of his dislike of leftist political movements makes itself felt.
There can be no doubt but that Singer views socialism and communism as antithetical, first to the interests of the Jews, then to

the interests of society, and ultimately to those of humanity itself. It is significant that Singer endows an antileftist character named Lapidus with some of the classic utterances of the novel even though he appears in but a single scene and has no role whatever in the action. Lapidus disturbs the smug humanitarianism of the circle of Jewish leftists gathered at Gina Genendel's by pointing out that they weep bitter tears over every Ivan, every Slav, every oppressed nation of the world, except the Jews. He recounts an experience he had in Siberia which epitomized the self-deceptive masquerade of Jews who seek a substitute religion for the one they have deserted: " '. . . I saw a bunch of Jews, with scrawny beards, black eyes—just like mine. At first I thought it was a *minyan* for prayers. But when I heard them babbling in Russian and spouting about the revolution—the S.R's, the S.D.'s, Plekhanov, Bogdanov, bombs, assassinations—I started to howl' " (62).

Lapidus lashes these Jews who are eager to spill their ink and their blood lavishly for the liberation of every oppressed group except their own because, in strict accordance with Socialist doctrine, they deny the existence of the Jews as a people and so undermine their right to exist at all. Some deep-seated impulse of treachery leads these "emancipated" Jews to deny only to the people from which they have sprung those human rights which are indivisible from national rights. Bernard Lazare once wrote of emancipated French Jews that "it isn't enough for them to reject any solidarity with their foreign-born brethren; they have also to go charging them with all the evils which their own cowardice engenders. . . . Like all emancipated Jews everywhere, they have also of their own volition broken all ties of solidarity."[2] Lapidus foresees the most extreme consequences for the Jewish people arising from the fact that " 'We dance at everybody's wedding but our own' " (61). He, like Abram, is a Zionist who sees no solution to the anomaly of Jewish existence in an increasingly antisemitic Europe but "a corner of the world for our own" (62).

We should keep in mind that Singer has set the early part of the novel in the beginning of this century, at a time when Jews were reeling from two catastrophic disillusionments, one from the East and another from the West. In Russia, the peasants and workers in whose name the 1905 Revolution, with the massive involvement of Jewish intellectuals, had been made, joined in brutal pogroms against Jews; moreover, the Russian Socialist intellectuals after whom Jewish Socialists modeled themselves seemed to approve the pogroms. I. L. Peretz said that the message of these Russian revolutionists to the Jews, could they only have understood it, was this: "Pay everywhere the bloodiest costs of the process of liberation, but be unnamed in all emancipation proclamations. . . . You are the weakest and the least of the nations and you will be the last for redemption."[3]

In France, from 1894–99, a Jewish community which prided itself on its emancipation and equality before the law found itself engulfed by the antisemitism occasioned by the Dreyfus Affair, in which a Jewish officer of the General Staff was falsely accused and convicted of espionage for Germany. The emancipated, westernized French Jews responded not by defending Dreyfus or attacking antisemitism but by ostentatiously dissociating themselves from their unassimilated eastern brethern. They resisted the efforts of Clemenceau to help because he saw the Jews as an oppressed people and they refused to recognize that antisemitism was even involved. That is, they refused with one exception. According to Hannah Arendt, the only visible result of the affair "was that it gave birth to the Zionist movement—the only political answer Jews have ever found to antisemitism and the only ideology in which they have ever taken seriously a hostility that would place them in the center of world events."[4]

The point which is made by Lapidus and Abram Shapiro has to do not only with the personal failings, the inherent treachery of emancipated Jews who blind themselves to the meaning, or even the existence, of antisemitism; it has to do with the survival of the Jewish people. Why, they ask, should Jews relinquish their identity in order to assimilate with "humanity"? In fact, they argue, if assimilation were successful, it would merge the Jewish people not with all humanity but only with the Polish people, so that the division and strife of nations would continue as before, but the people of Israel would disappear from the earth.[5] But assimilation, as the novel fully demonstrates, proved impossible in Poland in any case.

For the older characters in the novel, like Abram Shapiro, or even the much younger Asa Heshel, Zionism is, as Theodor Herzl once said, "a return to the Jewish people even before it is a return to the Jewish homeland."[6] It is not accidental that Asa's first Zionist utterances in the novel come on the occasion of his return from

Switzerland to Tereshpol Minor. Upon entering the synagogue, Asa is overcome by "a heavy odor that seemed . . . to be compounded of candle wax, fast days, and eternity. He stood silent. Here in the dimness everything he had experienced in alien places seemed to be without meaning. Time had flown like an illusion. This was his true home, this was where he belonged. Here was where he would come for refuge when everything else failed" (237). This feeling of homecoming appears to be dependent on religion, yet when Asa tries to explain his feelings to his grandfather what he says is that Jews are a people like every other people, and are now "demanding that the nations of the world return the Holy Land to them" (238). The conjunction of the two passages is striking. Very soon there will be no Tereshpol Minor synagogue in which to seek refuge when all else fails, as it does, and the Zionist contention that the Jews of Europe are building on sand will be borne out.

Asa eventually loses his faith in Zionism, as in everything else. He does not become disillusioned with it, but his firsthand observation of the Bolshevik Revolution convinces him that all moral barriers to brutalization and massacre are now down, and that the powerlessness of the Jews will make them prey to the antisemitism of the nations even when they have their own land.

It remains for the generation of Asa's children, and his sister's, and Koppel's, to translate the desire for a return to the Jewish people into practical Zionism. Shosha, one of the four daughters Koppel had fathered with his first wife Bashele, marries an authentic Zionist pioneer named Simon Bendel, who clearly represents the most vital element of the youngest generation of Polish Jews in the novel. Singer's desire to single out Zionism from among the myriad political movements which contend with each other for the loyalties of Jews who are disaffected from traditional religion is evident in his treatment of Simon and his beleaguered group of Hebrew-speaking agriculturists: "Everyone was against them—the orthodox Jews, the Socialist Bundists, the Communists. But they were not the kind to be frightened off. If the Messiah had not come riding on his ass by now, then it was time to take one's destiny into one's own hands" (466). By the end of the novel many characters who had previously been indifferent or hostile to Zionism are flocking to Palestine, but theirs is the desire for survival rather than rebirth, and thus not essentially different from that of the Jews who try to flee to America.

From the point of view of orthodox Judaism, Zionism is objec-

tionable because it aspires to preempt the role of the Messiah:
" 'What's bothering you, rabbi? We are building a Jewish
home. "Except the Lord build the house, they labor in vain that
build it" ' " (466). There is here no debate, such as we witnessed
in *Satan in Goray*, about the desirability of hastening the arrival
of the Messiah by aggravating the evil situation of humanity so that
the Messiah may come to a generation steeped in sin. Almost everybody apart from the Communists recognizes that this would be
carrying coals to Newcastle. The Zionists seek to take upon themselves the task reserved by religious tradition for the Messiah because they sense that modern antisemitism is not merely another
form of religious Jew-hatred but the instrument of a pan-European
conspiracy to destroy the Jewish people. Moreover, Zionists are
unlikely to believe that the evil of the world is an instrument of the
divine omnipotence to bring forth good.

The entire novel is animated by a tremendous pressure toward
some apocalyptic resolution of the worsening condition of the Jews
of Europe. Early in the book, before either of the world wars has
taken place, it seems to the Orthodox that things cannot get worse
than they are:

Speakers were thundering that Jews should not wait for Messiah to come,
but build the Jewish homeland with their own hands. . . . The truth was
that the Jews were being persecuted more and more. Day by day it became
harder to earn a living. What would be the end of it all? There was only
one hope left—for Messiah to come, to come quickly while there were still
a few pious Jews left. (166)

During the First World War it seems even more certain to such as
Rabbi Dan Katzenellenbogen that the cup must at last be full. What
can be the meaning of the "endless wars" of the Gentiles and the
endless suffering of the Jews but that redemption is at hand?
" 'Enough! It is time! High time for the Messiah!' " Even the fabric
of daily life is permeated by the web of Messianic expectation in
the novel, so that Adele's delivery pains provoke the comment that
"everything is attended by suffering . . . birth . . . Messiah. . ."
(341). But with the approach of Hitler even many of the pious go
off to Palestine, and younger Chasidim complain about their elders
and their God: " 'The old generation knows only one thing: Messiah
will come. God knows, he's taking his time' " (530).

The approach of Hitler forces other changes of vision as well. The fearful disunity of the Jewish people, the disintegration of the Jewish community that Singer has traced through the essentially private lives of a myriad of characters who have sought to define themselves without regard to their Jewish identity, is mocked by the antisemitic myth according to which all Jews form a single cohesive unit working for domination of the world. " 'Jews are all Bolsheviks, bankers, Masons, Wall Street Speculators. All the sins of the world they ascribe to us. The others are pure white spotless lambs. Trotsky, Rothschild, and the rabbi of Ger all sit down to eat Sabbath pudding together' " (533). Yet even now, when all the Jews recognize that their various individual attempts to escape from their people's collective fate have been futile, only Abram draws the conclusion that " 'we should at least stick together.' " " 'Why?' " asks Asa Heshel, " 'We don't love one another that much' " (535).

The culminating event of the novel is the last Passover to be celebrated by the Jews of Warsaw before they and their civilization are buried in universal darkness. The celebration looks backward to the great holiday occasions earlier in the novel, when the spiritually dispersed members of what had formerly been the community of Israel are briefly united with their people and with their best selves; and it also looks forward to the yawning emptiness of the Jewish future in Europe. So insistent is Singer on the irresistibility of Jewish fate that for this Passover celebration he even goes to the trouble of recalling, from Palestine as well as America, those characters who have already emigrated, despite the fact that all the Jews still resident in Poland "were possessed of the same thought: to be helped to get out of Poland while there was still time" (566).

At first the holiday seems as different from the holiday occasions of the past as the Moskat grandchildren and greatgrandchildren seem from each other. Meshulam's son Pinnie, now an old man steeped in piety and eccentricity, marvels at the sight before him:

He had hardly realized that old Meshulam had left behind him such a multitude. But still it was not the same as in the old days. Then, when the family gathered at the old man's for the Chanukah holiday or Purim, they were all cut from the same cloth. But now Pinnie compared them in his mind to the animals and fowl of Noah's ark. There was such a bewildering variety of types: with beards and with shaven cheeks; yeshivah students and modern youngsters; women in matrons' wigs and women with naked hair. (566–67)

Leah, similarly, is astonished by the disparity in her own children:
"What a strange brood . . . a rabbi, an apostate, a teacher in a
college, a Wall Street lawyer!" (572). But Pinnie and Leah are
wrong. All the Jews are to be united by a common fate, for their
German murderers were to make no distinctions among them.

The Passover celebration, described in great, loving detail by
Singer, is the novel's most beautiful and most terrible occasion. Not
only does it summon up and reinforce the memory of past holidays;
it is a holiday on which the original redemption of the Jews from
bondage is commemorated and the hope of their imminent salvation
and return to their ancestral homeland is more immediate than at
any other time in the year. In a voice broken with weeping, Pinnie
recites: " 'And it is this same promise which has been the support
of our ancestors and of us, for in every generation our enemies have
arisen to annihilate us, but the Most Holy, blessed be He, has
delivered us out of their hands. . .' " (578). From the point of view
of Jewish religion Hitler was but a repetition of the Pharaohs and
Hamans and Chmielnickis who had plagued the Jews throughout
their existence. Yet many at the seder table wonder to themselves:
"Would a miracle happen this time too? In a year from now would
Jews be able again to sit down and observe the Passover? Or, God
forbid, would the new Haman finish them off?" For Asa Heshel,
however, neither Judaism nor Spinoza can make it plausible that
Hitler is part of the Godhead, and he therefore is convinced that
"They were all doomed" (578).

The Passover service traditionally concludes with the exclamation
"Next Year in Jerusalem," yet Singer pointedly omits any mention
of this in his description of the Passover seder, instead concluding
with Pinnie's question, " 'These unleavened cakes, why do we eat
them? . . .' " Even though the novel treats Zionism favorably and
in this chapter we are told that Asa's son David was observing the
Passover holiday in Palestine with his fellow pioneers, Singer does
not want to endorse the historicist view of the Holocaust as, in the
words of one historian, "an ineluctable stage in Jewish history—the
labour pains of national rebirth . . . or the price of redemption."[7]
On the contrary, Singer wants above all to give the sense that for
the Jews of Europe the end of the world was at hand, and in a more
absolute sense than any that could be conceived either by orthodox
religious Jews or by nationalist Jews. When Abram tries to console
the gloomy Asa by saying that " 'the end of the world hasn't come

yet,' " Asa replies that " 'the end of our world *has* come' " (535).
Moreover, the last word in the novel (at least in its English version[8])
is given to a view of the Messiah that has never before been expressed throughout this long book, either by Chasidim or Zionists,
a view which sees no apocalypse in disaster, no future beyond the
abyss of the immediate present. Asa Heshel, having just learned
that his first wife Adele has been sent back from Palestine, "like
garbage," by the British, and that his second wife Hadassah has just
been killed in the German bombardment of Warsaw, is astonished
by a friend, Hertz Yanovar, who says that " 'the Messiah will come
soon.' " But in fact Asa has no cause to be irritated by what he
mistakenly takes to be an expression of the stupid optimism of the
people of hope, for Hertz is quick to inform him that " 'death is the
Messiah. That's the real truth' " (611).

CHAPTER 4

The Magician of Lublin

How long halt ye between two opinions? if the LORD be God,
follow Him, but if Baal, follow him.
—Elijah, First Kings, 18:21

T HE Magician of Lublin is Singer's first novel in which the hero
is not the Jewish people or a particular Jewish community but
a very singular individual who has largely (but not entirely) cut
himself off from the Jewish community, and even from the very
idea of community. Singer is here primarily concerned not with the
historical fate of the Jewish people or with the inescapability of
Jewish destiny, but with the nature of the artist, the conflict between
the aesthetic and the moral life, the elusiveness of perfect freedom,
and the attempt to find in religion the answers to ultimate questions.

Yasha Mazur, descendant of a pious Jewish family, is an acrobat
and magician and Don Juan who travels throughout Poland giving
performances to an adoring public and forming alliances with yet
more adoring women, although he has at home a wholly admirable
and dutiful wife named Esther (a variant, it may be noted, of the
name Hadassah). Yasha, not surprisingly, is held in low esteem by
the Jewish community. He appears in the synagogue only on Rosh
Hashanah and Yom Kippur, and, when he is reproached for his
impious ways, always replies: " 'When were you in heaven, and
what did God look like?' "(4). Since there can, in his view, be no
evidence that God has ever revealed his will to man, he cannot see
why what people allege to be God's law should be binding on him;
neither does he wish to be bound.

Yasha is no atheist, however. On the contrary, he believes that
"God's hand was evident everwhere" (6). (This belief is expressed
frequently in the first half of the book in passages of lyrical celebration of the glories of nature, the one artist in the universe to
whom Yasha defers: "The fields grew golden, fruit ripened in the

60

orchards. Intoxicating earth aromas induced lassitude and an ethereal calm. 'Oh, God Almighty, You are the magician, not I!' Yasha whispered. 'To bring out plants, flowers and colors from a bit of black soil!' " (60).

Although Yasha comes from Lublin, which in this book is an image of stability within the world of turmoil at the end of the nineteenth century, he inhabits many different worlds, each of which sends its representative to Yasha's imaginative world in the form of a resident lover. In the world of entertainment, to which he is professionally linked, his mistress is, conveniently, Magda, a Gentile assistant of lower-class origin who has worked with him for eight years. In the town of Piask, he associates with, but does not join, a gang of Jewish thieves, and carries on an affair with Zeftel, the deserted wife of one of the thieves. In these two worlds, and by these two women, he is fully accepted and even superstitiously revered. A third world, which he aspires to enter, is that of the Gentile middle class, whose representative in the novel's romantic framework is Emilia, a professor's widow who will not give herself to Yasha except as his wife. To achieve this end, however, Yasha will have to do three things which his residual Jewish conscience opposes: Emilia (who is descended from the Catholic offshoot of Sabbatianism) demands that Yasha leave his wife, convert to Christianity, and acquire a great deal of money. Yasha's efforts to fulfill these three conditions determine the action of the novel.

But although Yasha inhabits, or at least frequents, these different worlds, he does not feel much more at home in them than he does in Jewish Lublin. He is essentially "always a stranger, here [Lublin] and in Warsaw, amongst Jews as well as Gentiles." He is, moreover, a stranger not only to others but to himself, a man who is as mystified by the forces and passions which rage within him as others are awed by his ability to unravel what to them seem mysteries of import: how to pick a lock, how to turn a somersault on a high wire, how to hypnotize people into doing his will.

Yasha's talent (which is also his curse) for being in many diverse worlds without belonging to any of them is traditionally that of the artist, and *The Magician of Lublin* is in large part an exploration of the antithesis between the ethos of the artist and that of the believing Jew or, more generally, the godly person. Yasha thinks of himself not as a mere entertainer, magician, or acrobat: "He was no street performer now, who drags about with an accordion and

à monkey—he was an artist" (21). Yasha's self-congratulatory use
of this label is one aspect of his ambition to penetrate the enlightened world of Western Europe, and his flatterers seem to know
that the label is meat and drink to him: " 'But you, Panie Yasha,
you're an artist!' " (131).

The essential resemblance between Yasha Mazur and the character of the artist, however, is revealed in Yasha's musing over the
reasons for his attraction to the society of criminals. Puzzled by his
ability to speak of Copernicus, Galileo, and the Talmud with Emilia
in the afternoon, and then of thievery and murder with the criminals
of Piask in the evening, Yasha concludes that his peculiar genius
derives from his assumption of diverse and various masks. "There
was always another role for him to play. He was a maze of personalities—religious and heretical, good and evil, false and sincere. He
could love many women at once." Yasha also believes that his genius
for living vicariously through a number of different selves, none of
them entirely coextensive with his own, is what supplies him with
the key that unlocks the mystery which resides in each human
being: "Everyone was like a lock, each with his own key. Only one
such as he, Yasha, could unlock all souls" (58). The significance of
this remark is fully revealed only late in the novel when Yasha's first
failure to open a lock both signals his failure as a criminal and
precipitates his rejection of the artistic for the Jewish ethos.

Partly because of his chameleonlike ability to assume many selves
without becoming any one of them, Yasha loses knowledge of his
true self and spends many agonizing moments groping for it. If, in
the world of art, multiplicity of selves is an advantage, in moral life
it is a distinct disadvantage. For here you have to know who and
what you are. In moral life, the principle of exclusion takes primacy
over that of inclusion, the principle of community over that of pure
free-spiritism. Inevitably, Yasha's yearning after total inclusiveness
and total freedom for himself injures those like his wife Esther,
whose lives depend upon the sanctities deriving from the ideas of
self-limitation and community. His ability to love many women at
once makes marriage a condition difficult for him to encompass.

Yasha also imputes his attraction to the life of indiscriminate
sexuality and the world of the criminal to a malady which has been
associated with the artist since at least the beginning of the nineteenth century: boredom. "Yasha lay quietly, amazed at his own
behavior. 'It's all because I'm so bored,' he said to himself" (37).

He repeatedly justifies his conduct to himself by viewing it as the only anodyne for his boredom, as if sexuality and crime were to the bored man what alcohol is to the drunkard. By depicting Yasha's boredom as a fundamental cause of h s immorality and near-criminality, Singer links him with the most destructive forces of the past one hundred years, during which time what Irving Howe refers to[2] as "the explosive power of boredom" led to the breakdown of traditional society and its restraints. "Yasha was well aware that his worst enemy was his ennui. To escape it, he had committed all of his follies. . . . It was the disease that bound the underworld to decent society—the card players in a thieves' den to the gamblers at Monte Carlo; the pimp from Buenos Aires to the drawing-room Don Juan, the cutthroat to the revolutionary terrorist" (129). Singer implies that if Yasha had continued unimpeded down that path on which he had begun, he would have joined the company of those modern artists—like Brecht and Céline—who sought to assuage their boredom by celebrating the violence and cruelty of the criminal class with which they were spiritually allied—an alliance which was to find in the Jews its chief victims.

If Yasha's conscious ambition is to become a successful artist applauded by the civilized world of Western Europe, then his unconscious dream is that of freedom from social and even human limitations. His yearning for perfect freedom is epitomized by his endlessly dreaming of "putting on a pair of wings and flying" (38). Both his wife and his mistress-assistant Magda complain that, in the latter's words, " 'we're stuck here but you roam about as free as a bird' " (42). Yasha's dream of flying epitomizes his desire to be a free spirit, untrammeled by the necessities of commitment, community, and morality. It is reenforced by his artist's desire to perform and to observe the effects of his performance. "Now, with a pair of artificial wings he flew over the capitals of the world. Multitudes of people ran through the streets, pointing, shouting and, as he flew, he received messages by carrier pigeon—invitations from rulers, princes, cardinals." The dream of flying is sometimes also a dream of power, even of power for good: "In his imagination he even led the Jews out of exile, gave them back the land of Israel, rebuilt the temple of Jerusalem" (61–62). But Singer suggests how little consonant is the artist's dream of freedom and glory with the burdens of moral action by leading Yasha into a synagogue shortly after he dreams this particular dream. Here Yasha finds himself

mystified by the sight of an elderly worshiper whose head is sprin-
kled with ashes. In fact, what he is witnessing is the service of Tisha
b'Av, the Jewish holiday which is dedicated to mourning the destruction of the Temple and the initiation of that very exile which
Yasha has just dreamed of ending.

Yasha is impeded in the attempt to realize all his ambitions by
what remains in him of his Jewish conscience and Jewish identity.
His relation to the Jewish community is ambivalent. At times he
views the community of believing Jews, whose life is circumscribed
by prescriptions, prohibitions, and piety, with awe, wonder, and
envy, yet with the distinct feeling that he is an outsider to it. But
the feeling of alienation is strangely blended with the feeling of
belonging: "Everything seemed new to him: the way the Jews recited the introductory prayers, how they donned the prayer-shawls,
kissed the fringed garment, wound the phylacteries, unrolled the
thongs. It was all strangely foreign to him, yet familiar. . . . He was
part of this community. Its roots were his roots. He bore its mark
upon his flesh" (66–67).

Each time Yasha contemplates the various demands made upon
him by Emilia—desertion of his wife, conversion to Christianity,
the acquisition of money—he is restrained from grasping what he
desires by the mysterious immanence, for him, of the Jewish religion. Sometimes this comes to him through smells, sometimes
through memories, sometimes through a sense of the sanctity that
still permeates a universe whose inhabitants are blind and deaf to
the voices and words that call to them: "In the ante-chamber he
saw a barrel filled with pages torn from holy books. . . . An exalted
scent arose from the tattered leaves as if, lying there in the barrel,
they had continued being read by themselves" (67). Although Yasha
has cut himself off from the living Jewish community, he is still
bridled and inhibited by the religion of his fathers because the
Jewish people are a community of the dead as well as of the living:
"He was descended from people of honor. His grandfathers. . .
were famous for their honesty" (84). It is on their account, and not
because he is convinced of the truth of the Jewish religion or the
intrinsic validity of the first, seventh, and eighth commandments,
that Yasha holds back from deserting Esther, converting to Christianity, and turning thief on Emilia's account. Yasha himself does
not always know exactly what is the origin of the barrier separating
him from those who seek joy from life, but Singer leaves little doubt

that what undermines Yasha's ambition and lust for life with a sense of the vanity of things and "a guilt that could neither be repaid nor forgotten" (96) is the Jewish ethos. Christian society, as depicted in the novel, is far more eclectic and assimilative than Jewish society.[3] Whereas Judaism seems to Yasha at war with art and joy and even worldly life—"the street and the synagogue denied each other"—Christian culture accommodates the arts, worldliness, and even sin itself. Logically this mixture should attract Yasha, for, if he could harmonize his diverse impulses instead of oscillating between them, he might find peace. Yet paradoxically it is precisely the integrating power of Christian culture that repels him. Aspiring to the fame and fortune which accrue to artists in the world of Western Europe, he is appalled to learn that the actress at whose feet all France worships is a whore: "Was this the culture, the art, the aestheticism that the journals wrote about with such fervor?" (94). Apparently Christian culture is able to accommodate and assimilate everything (except, of course, the Jew): "Artfully, they had fused religion with materialism, connubiality with adultery, Christian love with worldly hate" (99). Ill at ease in Zion, Yasha feels still more alien to Babylon.

Yasha viscerally resents and rejects the eclectic character of Christian culture because his characteristic vision of life is of a choice between extreme and mutually exclusive alternatives. When, early in the story, his wife, Esther, asks him to bridle his passions a little, he replies by asking, " 'What would happen if I became an ascetic and, to repent, had myself bricked into a cell without a door like that saint in Lithuania?' " (25). For him there is no middle way between debauchery and asceticism. When Esther argues that repentance is possible without self-imprisonment, Yasha's reply is that she cannot know this unless her strength of uncontrollable passion is as great as his. His imagination fluctuates between the dream of the perfect freedom of a bird and the total imprisonment of an ascetic who will not expose himself to the test of free will.

One of Yasha's last exercises of free will is his decision to commit the robbery which will supply the money he needs to marry Emilia and move with her and her daughter to Italy. He hopelessly bungles the crime and injures himself in his escape. At first he cannot credit what has happened, for the crime was thwarted by his failure—the first in his life—to pick a lock; nor was this lock at all in the class of the fantastically complicated contraptions he had opened for sport or in performance, but a neighborhood job, put together by an ordinary locksmith. So completely had Yasha lost possession of himself that he even left at the scene of the aborted crime some pages from his address book that he had used to form a cone which could probe the keyhole. Still more puzzling, the master of the high wire is unable to descend from a balcony. He seeks to support himself on (significantly) a work of art—the shoulders of a statue—but his legs are too short and he is forced to jump to the ground, thus injuring his left foot.

Yasha escapes his pursuers by taking refuge in a synagogue, where he finds the true explanation of the bungled theft. Offered prayer shawl and phylacteries, the tools of Jewish religion, Yasha cringes with shame at his utter inability to handle them, he who had once managed locks and high wires so deftly. Then suddenly it dawns on him that Heaven itself has thwarted his crime and thereby saved him from the consequences of his own worst impulses. This revelation leads him to cringe with shame for true causes, not because he is clumsy, but because his whole life has been a betrayal of his fraternity with his fellow Jews, whose love for him comes unbidden and unconditionally. In one of Singer's classical descriptions of penitence and return, Yasha remembers the deathbed promise his father had elicited from him that he would remain a Jew. Now, suddenly, "It was obvious that those in heaven did not intend to have him turn to crime, desert Esther, convert. Maybe even his deceased parents had interceded in his behalf." Yasha's failure to commit the crime becomes to him an incontrovertible sign that God still has a covenant with him, that God punished him so promptly precisely because he bore him a special love. Overwhelmed by the feeling that there is a God who watches and participates in the world of men and who desires them to repent, Yasha decides that "I must be a Jew!. . . A Jew like all the others" (152–153).

Yet this very characteristic passage of return (the Hebrew root from which the Yiddish word for penitence is derived means "return") is followed by what is for Singer an equally characteristic passage describing the cooling of piety which takes place when the would-be penitent moves from the synagogue into the street and ordinary life. For Yasha it is almost a contradiction in the nature of things that the Jews who a few minutes earlier had chanted with fervor, "Let the great name be blessed forever," should now be chanting, "Smoked herring!" and "Fresh bagels!" and "Hot eggs!"

Perhaps his failure to open the safe and his injury of his leg were due to nothing other than nervousness and exhaustion. He therefore asks God to perform another miracle, give him another sign. But what he then sees is a hideous cripple whose suffering moves Yasha to ask, "How can a merciful God permit a human being to suffer such torment?" (158).

Nevertheless, Yasha's experience has had its effect. He is now indifferent to all his former ambitions. Content henceforth to have "one God, one wife, like everyone else" (159), Yasha confesses his crime to Emilia, who—just as he had unconsciously hoped—rejects him for the crime he had committed on her account. (She had wanted the money, but not the criminality.) More than ever before he senses the unbridgeable gap between the ethos of the worldly artist and that of the Jew. He reads a Talmudic commentary which makes strict, indeed extreme demands upon him, particularly with respect to sexual indulgences, and contrasts it with the boundless tolerance of worldly writers for crime and sin: ". . . mere worldly writers demanded nothing. For all such authors cared, he could kill, steal, fornicate, destroy himself and others. He had often met literary men in cafes and theaters; they busied themselves kissing women's hands, bestowing compliments upon all and sundry; were constantly ranting against publishers and critics" (199).

Yasha moves in stages on the path to penitence. His revelation is sufficient to persuade him of the primacy of morality in life. But it is only gradually that he comes to understand the relation between morality and ritual. At first it seems difficult to understand the connection, if any, between the morality preached by the biblical prophets and the requirement that one pray three times a day, wear a fringed garment, and observe hundreds of other prescriptions. Yet Yasha knows that "he most certainly would not have been involved in all these love affairs and other escapades if he had put on a fringed garment and prayed thrice daily." Yasha had, after all, as we have noted earlier, worked out his own religion of nature, but now he knows that such a religion looks good only in fair weather: "An abstract faith inevitably led to sin" (198).

In his search for that form of faith most suitable to him, Yasha wanders into a Warsaw synagogue frequented by Lithuanian Jews, whose rationalistic religion was so different from that of the Chasidim Yasha was familiar with in Lublin. Theirs is hardly an "abstract" faith, yet Yasha is offended that they (like himself) are clean-shaven and wear modern dress. They too, in his eyes, are guilty of the sin of occupying a half-way house between the Lord and Baal, between total commitment and total anarchy. "What was the point in shaving the beard, then praying, he asked himself. . . . As long as one believed in God and the Torah, why compromise? If there was a God and His Law was true, then He must be served night and day" (195).

Yasha's intense conviction of the need for extreme commitment is now reenforced by two unmistakable signs of the folly and wickedness of his, and of all, worldly existence. His self-disgust already so great that it literally produces nausea, he returns to Magda's apartment to find his lover and collaborator dangling from the end of a rope. She has committed suicide, from jealousy of Emilia. Shortly after this horrible discovery, Yasha happens upon another of his mistresses, Zeftel, in bed with a white-slave trader named Herman. The "lovers" are in too deep a sleep to notice Yasha's presence, and in fact the lifelessness of their faces is indistinguishable from that of corpses, except for the man's snoring. The vision of these "two spent figures, two wornout puppets," fills Yasha with shame not for them but for himself, for "the humiliation of one who realizes that despite all his wisdom and experience, he has remained a fool" (220).

The intimate, almost causal linkage between adultery and murder is borne in upon Yasha (as upon so many of Singer's penitents). He feels himself to have been guilty of both, and his revulsion from worldliness is final and complete, for he recognizes that the violation of a single commandment is potentially the violation of all of them. "Twice in one day there had been unveiled to him things which are best concealed. He had looked on the faces of death and lechery and had seen that they were the same. . . . The last twenty-four hours were unlike any previous day he had experienced. They summed up all his previous existence, and in summing it up had put a seal upon it. He had seen the hand of God. He had reached the end of the road" (220).

Thus ends Yasha's worldly existence, and with it the novel proper. In the Epilogue we see Yasha three years later, in his new incarnation. He has been renamed Reb Jacob, the Penitent, and has had himself bricked into a small structure, which Esther calls a prison, in the courtyard of their house. The only contact between Yasha-Jacob and the outside world takes place through a tiny window cut into the doorless house. Despite rabbinical pleadings that human life takes all of its meaning from the drama of choice and free will, Yasha-Jacob opts out of this drama. For his exercise of free will and his pursuit of freedom had led him to violate every law of the Torah even as he deluded himself with the belief that he was a righteous man.

These arguments which take place between the rabbis and Yasha even after he has repented and taken upon himself the full burden of Torah Judaism as well as the accoutrements of beard, sidelocks, skull cap, and fringed garment, serve to emphasize the fact that Yasha's resolution of his life is not explicitly Jewish. Although Yasha's criminal ambitions were bridled by what remained in him of an inherited Judaism, he was brought to repentance by a very individual sense of sin. When he senses the inadequacies of abstract religion, it is only natural that he should choose Judaism as the form of his external discipline. But *The Magician of Lublin,* unlike most of Singer's novels, takes as its hero not the Jewish community but an individual, and poses as its central problem not the historical fate of the Jewish people but the inability of strong passion to find a resting place in between the extremes of debauchery and asceticism, perfect freedom and total imprisonment.

Never does Yasha waver in his conviction that man must choose between two extremes. "There was no middle road. A single step away from God plunged one into the deepest abyss" (230). When he was free, Yasha had aspired to the airborne freedom of the angels; now he believes that man is the opposite of an angel and must be treated as such: "A beast must be kept in a cage" (238). The cage is not a perfect resolution of Yasha's dilemma, however. At first he thinks that solitude banishes all externalities, and that "it was as if he had become again a foetus in his mother's womb. . ." (226). But soon he is again plagued both by religious doubt and sexual desire. The external transformation does not guarantee the internal, nor does his self-imprisonment save him from contact with the fools who still inhabit the world, for Yasha becomes as much a sought-after celebrity when a penitent as he had been when a magician.

Yasha's escape from the pitfalls inherent in the life of art and of the world is, then, imperfect. It saves him from further sinning, but not from temptation and doubt. But this should not mislead us into thinking that Singer is recommending a middle way between freedom and asceticism. If Singer were a humanist writer in, say, the tradition of Montaigne or Shakespeare, we could assume that he was demonstrating that the man who aspires to the condition of angels is likely to fall lower than that of beasts, that man needs a middle path between asceticism and self-abandonment. But in fact the novel neither offers nor implies any such solution. We have a depiction of two unsatisfactory (but not equally so) extremes, and from them we may, if we wish, infer a mean. Moreover, Yasha, even after he is aware of the imperfect character of his new self and existence, explains that he had to abandon the world because he "could no longer breathe" (236) there, a sentiment repeated by many a Singer penitent, most notably Ezriel Babad in *The Manor*. Singer wishes not so much to undercut the thrust of the first nine-tenths of the book as to show that at least one of the convictions of the unregenerate Yasha was correct: to the ultimate questions there are no easy and absolute answers.

CHAPTER 5

The Slave

And Ruth said: "Entreat me not to leave thee, and to return from following after thee; for whither thou goest, I will go; and where thou lodgest, I will lodge; thy people shall be my people, and thy God my God; where thou diest, will I die, and there will I be buried; the LORD do so to me, and more also, if aught but death part thee and me."

—Ruth 1:16–17

THE story told in *The Slave* (1962) is classically simple, far more so than that of any other Singer novel. It is broken into three parts, respectively entitled "Wanda," "Sarah," and "The Return." In Part One Jacob, the hero, is shown living as a Jewish slave among savage peasant mountaineers. At the time of the Chmielnicki massacres, the most terrible in the sixteen-hundred-year history of Diaspora Jewry, Jacob had been twenty-five, a teacher with a wife and children. But they had been killed by the Cossacks, and Jacob, a survivor, had been sold into slavery. When we meet him, he is twenty-nine, the slave of Jan Bzik and the object of the affections of Bzik's daughter Wanda, the widow of a drunken peasant but herself sufficiently distinguished from the savages among whom she lives to have been nicknamed, more than half derisively, "The Lady." Jacob could escape his bondage and become an equal member of the village in which he lives if he would forsake his Judaism. But this he steadfastly refuses to do, and despite his isolation among strangers remains faithful to the Jewish God and to his law, the 613 commandments of which he undertakes (in imitation of Moses himself) to inscribe on stone. After long restraint, he finally succumbs to physical passion and is seduced by Wanda, though it is already clear that her "lust" is as much for knowledge of the Jewish God as for the flesh of Jacob. Jacob converts her to Judaism, though he is plagued by the suspicion that her desire to accept his faith has

71

come from "impure" motives and that therefore she has been im-
properly converted. Not long after this unusual marriage and conversion, Jacob is ransomed by his fellow Jews and brought back to
his ravaged home town, Josefov. But his heart remains with Wanda,
to whom he returns so that he may rescue her from savagery and
return with her to the Jewish community.

In Part Two, Wanda emerges re-created as "Dumb Sarah," the
mute wife of Jacob the schoolteacher in the village of Pilitz, a Jewish
community which has burgeoned on the edges of the manor of Adam
Pilitzky, a dissolute Polish nobleman. Sarah pretends muteness
because her imperfect Yiddish would very likely reveal her Gentile
origins, and Polish law punishes by death the "crime" of converting
a Gentile to Judaism. But, in the throes of terrible labor pains,
Sarah reveals her identity, and also reviles the false Judaism of Pilitz
which has from the first prevented the community from accepting
her. Jacob, who had achieved considerable eminence in the community as well as high favor from Adam Pilitzky and his wife, is
disgraced and once again enchained after Sarah's death. In the
course of his flight he meets an emissary from the Holy Land, who
urges him to go there because the Messiah (Sabbatai Zevi) is near
at hand. But first Jacob slips back into Pilitz to carry off his new-
born child Benjamin, who, like the first Benjamin, is a *ben-oni*, a
"child of sorrow."

In Part Three, which takes place twenty years later and is by far
the shortest segment, Jacob returns from *Eretz Israel* to retrieve
the bones of Sarah and take them for reburial on the Mount of
Olives in Jerusalem. We now learn that both he and his son, despite
their exemplary and unswerving piety, were almost ensnared by
Sabbatai Zevi and that Jacob nearly followed the example of the ill-
fated false messiah, who converted to Islam. But once again, as so
often in his life, Jacob resisted the temptation "to return to Egypt"
and did not desert the tree of life which is Torah. Although his son
Benjamin, who in the view of the old community of Pilitz had not
even been a Jew, is now an instructor in a Jerusalem yeshiva and
the son-in-law of a rabbi, Jacob is still spurned by most of the Pilitz
Jews. He dies in the Pilitz poorhouse, failing in his mission to rebury
Sarah in Jerusalem but joining her in the local graveyard, most
fitting symbol both of Jewish history and the Jewish future in Poland.

Despite its surface simplicity and the fact that only Jacob and
Wanda-Sarah are fully developed characters, *The Slave* is one of

Singer's most ambitious works of fiction. Although it is set, and with some degree of concreteness, in a post-1648 Poland reeling from the effects of Cossack butchery, it has also a vast backward and forward reference. It looks backward to the Bible, especially to the warfare between nascent Judaism and ancient idolatry, and forward to the Holocaust. The novel also undertakes, by tracing the fate of a Jew who involves himself in endless misfortune as a result merely of saving one gentile soul from the darkness of idolatry, to fathom the nature of Judaism itself, and the extent to which the living Jewish community has departed from those transcendent ideals by which it traditionally defined and disciplined itself.

The peasants among whom Jacob is exiled in Part One of *The Slave* are not to be thought of as Christians, except in the most superficial sense. If the local priest Dziobak were filled with an evangelical zeal to convert the heathen to Christianity, he would be far more usefully occupied in tending to the "Christian" peasants than to the heretic Jacob against whom he fulminates. For Jacob, the peasants are barely distinguishable, in their hygienic and sexual habits, from beasts. Neither cleanliness nor godliness seems to have recommended itself to them. They wallow in filth, copulate when and where they please and with whomever they can subdue. Their religion is not Christianity but witchcraft. Wanda is struck by the way in which Jacob's religion converts nature to human purposes instead of worshiping it. "Her family conducted themselves like animals. It hadn't occurred to any of them that the stream that flowed before their house could be used for bathing. It was the same one that passed near Jacob's barn" (30).

The first of a series of biblical archetypes in the novel establishes the peasants (or Gazdas) as a collective Esau in opposition to Jacob, who never ceases to wonder that he shares the human status with these debased creatures. "The men hee-hawed and whinnied, supported themselves on each other's shoulders, and barked like dogs. Some collapsed on the path, but their companions did not pause to assist them, but stepped over the recumbent bodies. Jacob was perplexed. How could the sons of Adam created in God's image fall to such depths?" (56–57). The son of the local bailiff, Stephan, is a true representative of this community in that "he was a man filled with iniquity like Esau or Pharaoh. Ever since Wanda could remember he had spoken of little else but killing and torturing" (79). Nevertheless, Jacob will have to admit—as his religion requires him to do—that Esau too had come from the seed of Abraham and Isaac. This makes the conversion and redemption of Wanda both possible and desirable.

Through his depiction of the polar opposition between the pagan Polish peasants and the Jewish slave Jacob, Singer hopes to achieve several purposes. Jacob's stubborn clinging to the Jewish God in opposition to idolatry is first of all a recreation of the struggle of the Jews of the Bible to resist, at the cost of their physical well-being and often their lives, the abominations and cruelty of idolatry. It is perfectly "natural" that these peasants should fear only one thing more than they fear vampires and succubuses: and that one thing is Jacob, the Jew. Jacob understands that his survival as a human being depends precisely on his submission before something that is more than human, a transcendent God and His law, a law which can raise men above themselves because it comes from a place above them. The only way that Jacob, a wanderer among idolaters and murderers, has of rescuing his soul is to scratch the commandments of God's law on a stone. The stone, moreover, is ready to hand because Jacob is reenacting the struggle of his forefathers to save themselves from the ultimate slavery of idol-worship: "He did not have to search far. Behind the barn a large rock protruded from the earth. There it stood as ready as the ram which Father Abraham had sacrificed as a burnt offering instead of Isaac. The stone had been waiting ever since Creation" (39). So convinced is Jacob that the savages among whom he lives are the incarnation of the followers of Baal, Astoreth, and Moloch that he for the first time in his life comes to accept the previously intolerable fact that the God of the Bible, the father of mercy, had demanded the slaying of entire peoples: "Now that Jacob observed this rabble he understood that some forms of corruption can only be cleansed by fire." (57).

The conflict between Jacob and his pagan surroundings also serves to illuminate the relationship between Judaism and Christianity, especially in Poland. Dziobak, the local priest, outdoes his pagan flock in hatred of Jacob and indeed urges the murder of the Jew in disregard of Jan Bzik's wish to protect his slave. His actions are almost a parabolic representation of the peculiar venom of Polish antisemitism. Christianity came to Poland relatively late, in 966, and the Polish Church was therefore all the more fearful that the presence of a prosperous minority population of a different faith would keep Christianity from taking root. In 1267, the Church

Council of Breslau declared: "In view of the fact that Poland is a *nova plantatio* [a new planting] in the body of Christianity, there is reason to fear that her Christian population will fall an easy prey to the influence of the superstition and evil habits of the Jews living among them, the more so as the Christian religion took root in the hearts of the faithful of these countries at a later date and in a more feeble manner."[1]

The unceasing policy of hatred, discrimination, and violence pursued over centuries by the Polish Catholic Church toward Jews is accurately reflected, then, in Dziobak's relation to Jacob. Yet both Jacob and Wanda recognize that Judaism and Christianity are closer to one another than to paganism. Jacob understands that from the point of view of Judaism Christianity is preferable to paganism because it has at least a drop of Torah mixed in with all its Greek mystery religion. Wanda, from the pagan side, would find Jacob's ethical precepts totally alien to her if they did not strike her ear in something like the way that Dziobak's words (though never his actions) had done.

The intrinsic beauty and worth of Judaism appear most strikingly in the first part of the book, in which Wanda's "Jewish soul" strives to break free from its pagan entrapments by uniting with Jacob. "She lusted for knowledge almost as fiercely as she did for the flesh" (83). Jacob is constantly surprised by the intelligence and immediacy of Wanda's questions about the Jewish God, who is also the God of all mankind. The more she hears of this religion of distinction, of prohibitions, of restraints, of subduing nature to history, the more she feels that until now she has had no eyes. " 'I believe, Jacob. Honestly I do. But you must teach me. Without you I am blind' " (83).

Although he has been seared by tragedy, Jacob is still sufficiently bound by the yoke of the covenantal idea of Jewish religion to believe that "God had punished His people and had hidden his face from them, but He continued to superintend the world" (8). Jacob can answer Wanda's curious inquiries because he believes, like generations of Jews before him, that the terrible sufferings of the Jews had been inflicted on them because of their sins and were not a revelation that God had in fact deserted them or was impotent to protect them.

But no sooner is Jacob ransomed and brought back to live among the Jews of Josefov than he is cast into doubt, and Judaism looks far less worthy and beautiful than it did in exile among the idolators. In Josefov, his intelligence and his imagination are assaulted by the enormity of suffering which the Jews there (as elsewhere in Poland) have endured at the hands of Chmielnicki's Cossack revolutionaries. In reply to his inquiry about who is left alive in Josefov, "every sentence ended with the word 'killed.' . . . Yes, the Angel of Death had been busy. The massacres and burnings had been followed by sickness, and people had died like flies. Jacob found it difficult to comprehend so much calamity." The God of history whose ultimate wisdom and justice Jacob had so eloquently expounded to Wanda had apparently absented himself from the world at the time of the Jews' greatest need. "The explanation he had given Wanda that free will could not exist without evil nor mercy without sorrow now sounded too pat, indeed almost blasphemous. Did the Creator require the assistance of Cossacks to reveal His nature? Was this a sufficient cause to bury infants alive?" (101–102).

This section of the book, in which Jacob is assailed by horrifying accounts of the obscene violation and massacre of his own flesh and blood, resonates with the questions raised by the Holocaust itself, of which the Chmielnicki massacre is a type: " 'Why did this happen to us?' one of the men asked. 'Josefov was a home of Torah.' 'It was God's will,' a second answered. 'But why? What sins did the small children commit? They were buried alive.' " How, asks Jacob, can the mind grasp such a quantity of horrors? "There was a limit to what the human mind could accept. It was beyond the power of any man to contemplate all these atrocities and mourn them adequately." Could Chmielnicki really be a part of the godhead or was it perhaps true that this massacre of the Jews revealed the existence of a radical evil in the universe, a devil who had no celestial origins? *The Slave* also shows us Jews who are forced to dig their own graves before they are executed; berates the Jewish community for its shameful failure to offer forceful resistance to murderers; and preaches the sacred duty of remembering forever those who were slaughtered. "Through forgetfulness," thinks Jacob, "he had also been guilty of murder" (102–103). In its dwelling upon the physical obscenities of the mass murders, *The Slave* may even be said to deal more concretely with the Holocaust than those novels and stories by Singer which approach it frontally.

But it is not only accounts of unfathomable suffering which unsettle Jacob's faith. His expectation that the saving remnant, be-

lieving that their own sins had been the true cause of their
misfortune, would now lead the purest of lives, proves mistaken.
Virtue is not schooled by suffering. When Jacob was distant from
all Jews, he loved them wholeheartedly. But now that he has rejoined them he is afflicted by their pettiness, their deviousness,
their quarrelsomeness. Among savages, he had been certain of his
faith; back among the Jews, "he doubted everything. . ." (119).

What particularly occasions his doubt is the disparity he observes
between strict observance of *halachic* regulations and utter indifference to the must fundamental ethical obligations. ". . . As Jacob
looked about him, he saw that the community observed the laws
and customs involving the Almighty, but broke the code regulating
man's treatment of man with impunity. . . . Yes, men and women
who would rather have died than break the smallest of these ritu-
alistic laws, slandered and gossiped openly, and treated the poor
with contempt." The moral inefficacy of *halachic* Judaism reflects
a disillusionment which runs very deeply and strongly through the
book. Jacob now sees that "one law in the Torah generated a dozen
in the Mishnah, and five dozen in the Gemara." During his years
of absence many additional prohibitions had been added to the
Shulchan Aruch, the code of Jewish observance. "A wry thought
occurred to him: if this continued, nothing would be kosher. What
would the Jews live on then? Hot coals?" (117–118).

But it is not until Part Two of the novel that the deepest inadequacies of this debased ghetto Judaism are revealed. For the
"Dumb Sarah" whom Jacob brings as his wife to Pilitz has been
converted under the aegis of the pure, biblical, and (this most of
all) "prophetic" Judaism of Jacob. Sarah had been born with "a
Jewish soul" (287) and her instruction in Judaism had been endowed
with that purity which is perhaps only possible in isolation from a
living community and its endless imperfections. The Judaism of
Sarah, taught her by Jacob, is that of the Ten Commandments and
of the prophetic exhortation to deal justly with one's fellow men,
rather than the religion of legalisms and rituals. It is therefore the
severest kind of judgement on the Jewish community of Pilitz that
it cannot accept Sarah in its midst. The Jewish women of Pilitz
mistreat her even before they know she is a convert, partly because
she is (or rather pretends to be) a mute and is therefore unworthy
of so splendid a specimen as Jacob, partly because, although she
is strictly observant of Jewish law, her manners are alien to them.

It is therefore not only external pressure but internal weakness which prevents this Jewish community from accepting a convert. The question of conversion to Judaism is central in the novel, which explores it from several different points of view. Singer knows that, contrary to modern propaganda (Jewish as well as Christian) on the subject, Judaism was once a proselytizing religion and could well become one again. The two salient facts about conversion which Jacob often repeats stolidly to Wanda at first are that one cannot become a Jew unless one believes in God and His Torah, and that if a Christian becomes a Jew the Christian rulers of Poland will burn him at the stake. Later on, however, after he has cohabited with her and been ransomed away from her father, he allows his mind to play more freely over the subject. Was not the chemistry of human motivation far more complex than the rules allowed for? Were all those who over the centuries had become Jews by choice—and good Jews, too—moved solely by faith? Besides, "which was the greater transgression, the abandonment of one's issue to the idolaters or the conversion of a woman lacking a true vocation?" Still later, after Wanda's conversion into Sarah, Jacob hears the story of a whole band of Cossacks who told a Jewish woman they had kidnapped during the pogroms: " 'We want to become Jews' " (206). The emissary from Palestine whom Jacob meets after Sarah's death tells him that " 'before the Messiah will come, all the pious gentiles will have been converted' " (266).

But none of these possibilities can penetrate the consciousness of the Jews of Pilitz, especially its communal leaders. None of *them* appears to remember that Moses had taken an Ethiopian as his wife, and that when Miriam slandered him for this she became leprous. When Sarah reports to Jacob the slander directed against them, he assures her that " 'all those who gossip, ridicule, or speak evil of others, will burn in the fires of Gehenna' " (161). When the story of Sarah's conversion is revealed, the Jewish community invokes its terror of the death penalty it would receive from the Poles as an excuse for the rejection of Sarah which had already been decided upon for reasons having nothing to do with the threat of the Christians. The three themes of conversion, of the shortcomings of *halachic* Judaism, and of the true nature of Jewish religion, converge on Sarah's death-bed. Now, with nothing to hide, she can at least speak the truth to her tormentors: " 'You call yourself Jews but you don't obey the Torah. You pray and bow your heads but

you speak evil of everyone and begrudge each other a crust of
bread' " (227–28). The only benefit Jacob derives from Sarah's death
and his own excommunication is a revelation of the true nature of
Torah: "But now he at least understood his religion: its essence was
the relation between man and his fellows. Man's obligations toward
God were easy to perform. Didn't Gershon have two kitchens, one
for milk, and one for meat? Men like Gershon cheated, but they
ate matzoth prepared according to the strictest requirements. They
slandered their fellow men, but demanded meat doubly kosher.
They envied, fought, hated their fellow Jews, yet still put on a
second pair of phylacteries. Rather than troubling himself to induce
a Jew to eat pork or kindle a fire on the Sabbath, Satan did easier
and more important work, advocating those sins deeply rooted in
human nature" (247).

This critique of a debased Judaism would fit very well into the
familiar Christian pattern which claims that Christianity has in fact
become the true Israel and that Christians have superseded Jews
as God's elected people. But there is nothing in the novel to support
this claim, and in fact the unbreachable wall of an ethical imperative
bars the way to Christianity. To be sure, "God's wrath poured down
on his people. But the moment the Jews caught their breath, they
returned to Judaism. What else could they do? Accept the religion
of the murderer?" (148). For Adam Pilitzky, the endless sufferings
of the Jews makes a mockery of their chosenness: " 'What has he
chosen you for? To live in dark ghettos and wear yellow patches' "
(184). But Jacob has only to look about the Pilitzky castle to see the
contrast between the inheritance of Esau and that for which he and
his ancestral namesake were chosen: "Everywhere were trophies
of the hunt . . . . In the armory were displayed swords, spears,
helmets. . . . The very air of the castle smelled of violence, idolatry,
and concupiscence" (193). If you joined Esau, you might not be
among the murdered in the next pogrom, but you could be among
the murderers.

But although Jacob knows that this way can never be his, everything that befalls him and his people forces upon him the question
of whether the Jews can survive at all if they do not stoop to pick
up Esau's sword (though not his idolatrous worship of it). The book
takes for granted the view that Diaspora Jewry had crippled itself
by its pacific ethos. "Stories he had heard of how the Jews had
behaved during the massacres shamed him. Nobody had dared lift

a hand against the butchers while they slaughtered entire communities. Though for generations Jewish blacksmiths had forged
swords, it had never occurred to the Jews to meet their attackers
with weapons. The Jews of Josefov, when Jacob had spoken of this,
had shrugged their shoulders. The sword is for Esau, not for Jacob"
(268). But here again Wanda, schooled by Jacob in the religion of
the Bible, knows that Jews did not always behave this way. Jacob's
growing resentment of this passivity becomes evident in a scene
where the odious Pilitzky is publicly humiliating the (equally odious)
leader of the Jewish community, Gershon, and the Jews, though
greatly outnumbering Pilitzky's servants, "just stood gaping with
legs spread wide, amazed. . . at their own impotence" (167). Jacob
alone steps forward to defy the Gentile oppressor.

But it is not until very late in the story, when Jacob is being led
away in chains by the authorities because of his involvement in the
criminal act of converting a Christian to Judaism, that he resorts to
violence. "Suddenly it occurred to Jacob that sometimes chains
could be broken. Nowhere was it written that a man must consent
to his own destruction" (251). Upon the very instant of this recognition Jacob grasps the means to escape his captors and save his
life. For the rest of his life, we are told, he "heeded the advice of
the Book of Aboth: 'If one comes upon thee, to kill thee, rise first
and kill him' " (270). This advice proves eminently useful in Jacob's
new life in *Eretz Israel*, where, we learn, "he dared defy armed
Arabs or Turks" (296).

Excommunicated by his own people, pursued by the Poles, Jacob
finds himself left with nothing but his faith and the infant child of
his dead Sarah. In this state, he meets two providential messengers
who propose two antithetical paths to him. One is a kindly Gentile
ferryman named Waclaw, who insists that (as Jacob has good reason
to know) a virtuous life is nearly impossible in any organized community, and that marriage, family, religion are inevitably enslaving
and corrupting. The other is an emissary from the Holy Land who
tells him (contrary to Waclaw) to retrieve his child and go to settle
in the Holy Land. This is not only a great act of piety in itself. Jews
can breathe more easily there and, most compelling reason of all,
the Messiah is at hand. Jacob chooses the latter of the two paths
because he recognizes it as the one for which he has been destined:
"His name was Jacob also; he too had lost a beloved wife, the
daughter of an idolater, among strangers; Sarah too was buried by

the way and had left him a son. Like the biblical Jacob, he was crossing the river, bearing only a staff, pursued by another Esau. Everything remained the same: The ancient love, the ancient grief. . . . Perhaps it was always the same Jacob and the same Rachel. Well, but the Redemption has to come. All of this can't last forever" (278–79).

For the Jews of Poland, we know, this did *not* last forever. They became the victims of the first successful campaign of genocide in history. With the wisdom of hindsight (which is at least better than the stupidity of hindsight), Singer imagines a kind of alternative fate for Polish Jewry by dispatching his hero to the Land of Israel. To a common-sensical non-Sabbatian Jew of the seventeenth century, this could hardly—even in the aftermath of the Chmielnicki massacres—have seemed a practical solution. After all, he might have said to himself, if Jews and Judaism could not survive in Poland, the intellectual, religious, and biological center of Diaspora Jewry, where in the world could it survive? But Singer, writing with the dark knowledge of the Holocaust, knows that common sense would have been mistaken. Who but a man who had wrestled with God could imagine that in three hundred years from the time of Chmielnicki's pogroms there would be no Jews in Poland? Jacob is such a man.

Jacob's decision to go to the Holy Land is, to be sure, like that of hundreds who actually did go between 1696 and 1700, based on a gross delusion, the delusion that Sabbatai Zevi is the Messiah and that the long-awaited Redemption is at hand. But just as Jacob's marriage with Wanda had proved to be a godly act although done partly for selfish motives, so the commitment of his destiny to the Sabbatian movement in the Land of Israel, although springing from delusion, turns out to be an unalloyed gift of Heaven, bringing with it the blessing of a son who at age twenty is an instructor in a yeshiva and the son-in-law of a rabbi. Although Jacob, when he returns to claim Sarah's bones in Pilitz, curses the name and memory of Sabbatai Zevi, he does not doubt that in connecting himself with the historic Jewish community of Palestine, he has chosen life over death. "Not even Sabbatai Zevi had come in vain. False birth pains sometimes precede the true. Jacob, journeying through the Turkish countries from the Holy Land to Poland, had come to know things he had not understood before. Each generation had its lost tribes. Some portion always longs to return to Egypt." Pilitz *is* Egypt, and everything he sees there at the end of the story is redolent of death, as if the community had passed a final, fatal judgment on itself by the act of rejecting the convert Sarah. But despite all the death and all the destruction and all the treachery he has witnessed and suffered, Jacob dies consoled by the knowledge, given him by his survival and rerooting in the Holy Land, that although "The leaves drop from the tree, . . . the branches remain; the trunk still has its roots" (289–90). The odyssey of Jacob has not been from slavery to freedom. Even near the end of Part One, when he risks his newly-bought freedom to return to Wanda, we are told that Jacob "had passed beyond freedom" (139–40). Instead he has finally moved from the first to the second kind of "slavery" defined in *The Wisdom of the Fathers:* "Antigonus of Soko. . . used to say: Be not like slaves who serve their master for the sake of their allowance; be rather like slaves who serve their master with no thought of an allowance— and let the fear of heaven be upon you."

CHAPTER 6

The Manor *and* The Estate

With an effort which up till now has never been repeated I managed to
reach the cultural level of an average European. In itself that might be
nothing to speak of, but it is something insofar as it has helped me out of
my cage and opened a special way out for me, the way of humanity.

—The ape in Kafka's "A Report to
an Academy"

No group but the Jews so swiftly and irrevocably abandoned everything
for West European culture, discarded its religion, and divested itself of its
historical past and its traditions.

—Pauline Wengeroff (1833–1916)

*T*he *Manor* and *The Estate* (really a single novel in two parts)
portray the disintegration of Polish Jewry between 1863, the
year of the unsuccessful Polish insurrection against Russian domination, and the end of the nineteenth century. We watch the Jews
leave the small towns and ghettoes for the life of cosmopolitan
Warsaw and also Paris and New York. We watch them exchange
the long caftan and long hair of the Chasidim for the short jacket
and short hair (and often shortened memory) of the "modern" Jew,
who is sartorially then indistinguishable from the modern Gentile.
We witness the gradual substitution of Polish for the "jargon" of
Yiddish as the language of everyday speech. We see young men
who were brought up as Chasidim turn into Socialists, assimilationists, antisemites. We watch young women trained to be "pure
Jewish daughters" turn into Gentiles, or violent revolutionaries, or
adulteresses.

From one point of view, this is, as John Thompson has written,
"the oldest kind of story in the world, that of the destruction of a
human society, with all its ordered items of culture˙ arranged
through the centuries to bring meaning to every act of life—to make
life human."[1] In this sense, Singer's vast novel resembles works of
French or English or Russian literature which analyze the disin-

83

tegration of traditional culture. But in France or England or Russia the destruction of the traditional culture is (almost inevitably) accompanied by the burgeoning of a new culture which is still recognizable as French or English or Russian. The Jews of nineteenth-century Poland (or of any other time or place) did not have such a wide latitude. A Frenchman who rejected his father's religion and dress and manners would still remain, however transformed or diminished, a Frenchman—living on French soil, speaking the French language, even continuing, in secularized mode, the customs which for his parents were explicitly religious.

For the Jews of Europe, however, the loss of unity in religion meant the loss of Jewish identity itself. There were not a thousand ways of being Jewish, only one. This was partly a matter of circumstance, partly one of self-definition. Singer knows that the Jews have traditionally defined and disciplined themselves through the conviction that they were a holy people chosen by God to fulfill a special destiny. It was this inner compulsion which had enabled them to survive thousands of years in exile from their homeland while countless other nations, also subjected to defeat, exile, and oppression, had disappeared through assimilation. For the Jews of Europe to become, as we see them becoming in *The Manor* and *The Estate,* a worldly people, was for them to deny their own transcendent reason for being, their own life-principle. They could remain a nation in exile, a nation without a territory, only by adhering to their inherited religion and not—despite the valiant efforts of Jewish enlighteners, Jewish Socialists, and Yiddishists—in any other way.

The inflexibility of Jewish self-definition was an intellectual as well as a religious matter. One of the militant assimilationists of *The Estate* alleges that "in the hundreds of years that the Jews had studied nothing but the Talmud, the Gentiles had produced an Archimedes, a Euclid, a Copernicus, a Galileo, a Newton, a Pascal, and a Darwin. The Jews had stuck to ancient Talmudic precepts and the Gentiles had built railroads and steamships, had invented the telegraph and the telephone. . ." (E206. In this chapter, page references to *The Estate* are prefaced by E, and references to *The Manor* by M). The statement is extravagant, but not without some foundation in actuality. Judah Goldin has written that "at the root, and up through the branches and fruits, of all Jewish expression, is the persistent hum of the Hebrew Scriptures. . . . Until practically

the last century . . . the bulk of Jewish literature was essentially
commentary—in the countless polychromes it is capable of assuming. . . . You might say that all the principal creations of Jewish
literature—Bible, Midrash, Talmud, Responsa, Codes, Piyyut (Synagogue Poetry), Philosophy, Kabbala, Exegesis of the Bible and of
the post-biblical classics, Moralizing Chronicles and Treatises—all
the principal creations of this literature . . . join in one exclamation:
'Here is the design; it will be carried out; Man, what do *you* plan
to do about it?' "[2] Thus Jewish learning was neither liberal, which
is to say development of the intellect as a good in itself, sufficient
to rest in, nor servile, which is to say intended to produce "fruits,"
such as steamships and telephones. Rather it was an extended meditation on the question of how to live, how to make human life a
fitting prelude to life in the Messianic age. In the Book of Proverbs
and in the Jewish Prayer Book for the Sabbath, the vast body of
learning called "Torah" is called "a tree of life to those who take
hold of it." *The Manor* and *The Estate* deal in large part with the
fate of those who, in the interests of modernity or politics or science
or "universalism," cut themselves off from this tree of life and its
nourishment.

The Manor begins with the story of Calman Jacoby, a Jew who
has obtained a lease on the manor of Count Jampolski, who like
other Polish noblemen had been banished to Siberia by the Czar
after the unsuccessful rebellion of 1863. Calman, like Sholom Aleichem's Tevye, is burdened with daughters. He must marry off
four of them and in the process guarantee not only their material
well-being but the continuation of the Jewish traditions and values
he has inherited from his forefathers. His problems, however, are
not confined to the next generation. Ambitious, industrious, and
prosperous, he is forced again and again into situations which confirm the wisdom of a Talmudic saying: "The more property, the
more anxiety." Calman begins with the best of intentions, vowing
never to become like the rich men of Warsaw, who forsake God
and are forsaken by Him as they become inflated with their increasing wealth. Yet he is carried by the secular momentum of
riches and respectability into fancy clothing, a redecorated house,
and even the use of two things which to the Jews of Eastern Europe
were peculiarly Gentile properties: dogs and a gun. His wealth
strains his relations with his wife, who complains that he is now
rarely at home. Even in money matters, Calman finds that he is

worse off than before: "Strangely enough, he found that, as a man
of wealth, he was now deeply in debt, while as a poor man he had
not owed a cent" (M50).
Two other stories of families function as parallels to that of Calman
and his daughters. One is that of Count Jampolski himself, whose
social and financial decline is intimately linked with Calman's rise:
"Yes, Count Jampolski in his old age had divorced himself from all
luxuries while Calman, the Jew, had taken up residence in a palace,
amid gold, silver, porcelains, lackeys, and servants" (M242). Calman's most recalcitrant daughter, Miriam Lieba, follows her romantic star into the arms of the Count's son, Lucian, an egomaniac
and failed revolutionary; and both of the parents are outraged by
their children's marriage, the Count for social, Calman for religious
reasons.
    The more extended and convincing parallel subplot involves Reb
Menachem Mendel Babad, a rabbi who fathers two wayward children, Ezriel and Mirale. He, like Calman, associates big cities with
moral disorder and apostasy. This is why, early in the story, he
leaps at the chance to move his family from Lublin to Jampol, where
he has been offered the rabbinate. "Enlightened individuals," he
hopefully remarks, "could not possibly inhabit so small a community" (M25). Enlightenment is for him (as ultimately for the novel
itself) a pejorative term. He, like the Count, is linked with Calman
through marriage: he arranges for his son Ezriel to marry Calman's
daughter Shaindel. The parallel between the fortunes of Calman
and Menachem Mendel is not always in the foreground of the novel,
but it is never forgotten as a structuring principle. Thus both fathers
discover themselves to be "childless" at nearly the same point in
the story, when Calman's marriage to his youthful second wife Clara
has alienated him from Shaindel, Jochebed, and Tsipele, and Ezriel
and Mirale's separation from everything Jewish has divorced them
from their father.
    In the contrast between the older and younger generations in the
novel, physical appearance plays a large role. There is, of course,
no logical reason why this should be so, but life is not logic. For
the older people, the discarding of the skullcap and long capote and
side-curls was considered equivalent to apostasy. The old Yiddish
expression, "Zol im dos lebn farkirtst vern," that is, "May his life
be shortened" (like his coat), was, as Maurice Samuel has pointed
out,[3] the curse of a father against a sartorially rebellious son. The

young might protest that casting aside the standard outer garment
of the religious Jew was only a superficial change which removed
the external distinction between Jew and Gentile, but not the distinction by religion. In practice, however, the fathers were right,
the sons wrong: loss of distinction in "mere" externals usually meant
apostasy as well.

When we first meet Ezriel, the rabbi's son, he wears "full Hassidic
dress: skullcap, gaberdine, sash, and trousers tucked into high
boots." But his habits and his questions already reek of heresy. As
a boy, he had been attracted to "un-Jewish" pleasures like trapping
birds, bringing home "not only cats and dogs, but frogs and other
unclean reptiles." When the Sabbath was being prepared, he
thought not of its holiness but of the physical agonies of the carp
"scaled and cut to pieces for the Sabbath meal"; that is to say, he
put the naturalistic and "humane" consideration ahead of the divine
commandment. His questions about Scripture are of the sort Vol-
taire was wont to ask: Was Adam a Jew? Did Eve wear a bonnet?
Why does Scripture give contradictory accounts of the same event?
How could the revered King of Israel slay Uriah the Hittite? All
this, coupled with Ezriel's interest in physical science, leads his
father to the irresistible conclusion: "One began with questions,
then one adopted modern styles of dress, and next there was loss
of faith, even apostasy" (M 23–24).

The central character of this novel, as Mary Ellmann has pointed
out,[4] is Polish Jewry as a whole rather than Calman Jacoby or Ezriel
or any other character who stands in the foreground of the reader's
attention for long stretches, only to recede in favor of other characters who had previously lurked in the background. Singer has
invented dozens of characters and tried to follow the careers of each
one of them in such a way as to give us a panoramic survey of an
entire society, but of a society constantly in movement. In order
to achieve this, he employs a technique of what might be called
discontinuous presentation. After following a particular character
fairly closely through a considerable number of pages (and years),
he will drop the character for a long period of time and then pick
up the account of his or her life after a great many things have
happened without our witnessing them. This is partly a device of
economy, for if Singer had attempted to trace in detail the life of
every important character—and he makes us feel they are all important—the novel would have become unmanageable. It is also a

way of suggesting the nature of time, what it is and what it does to people, just as in actual life we more readily notice the changes wrought by time in persons we see only at widely spaced intervals. The technique could not, however, be convincing unless Singer had thoroughly persuaded us that his knowledge of all these characters is absolute. He omits the showing of certain things not because he does not know them or wishes to hide them from his reader, but precisely because he has endowed the reader with a fullness of knowledge which will give him the pleasure of fulfilled expectation rather than the shock of surprise when he discovers the fate of a character long absent from the story.

Because Ezriel is the character whose own story comes closest to being coextensive with that of the entire novel, it is worth paying close attention to his early life, for its course is a kind of introduction to the novel's main themes, which are echoed in lesser characters. His youthful interest in science is not only the fitting prelude to his later career as a neurologist, but the introducton of the naturalistic theme which pervades the book. Throughout *The Manor* and *The Estate* we find characters put to a hard choice between being religious and being animalistic. The conflict between Judaism and naturalism is absolute and allows of no resting-place in that halfway house called humanism. Calman, as soon as he is lured away from the traditional life of piety, finds himself wearing, instead of simple religious garb, "a fox-lined overcoat with little tails dangling from the inner seams" (M15). His new servant, the Gentile Antosia, was "in some ways . . . like an animal" (M18) and was as little embarrassed as an animal about inviting the married Calman to her bed. Count Jampolski does not have Calman's religion to restrain him when offered the same temptation: "He made no secret of the fact that he was cohabiting with Antosia, and Felicia heard the maid on her way to him each night. In his old age her father had turned into an animal" (M142).

This conflict between naturalism and religion is relentlessly pursued into the next generation, for whom Darwin affords the license to obliterate the distinction between man and animal. Wallenberg, the time-serving Jewish convert to Catholicism, offers Ezriel the use of his library of secular knowledge, particularly recommending " 'a recently published English book that is causing a furor in the world of science. Its theory seems to be that all life is a struggle for survival and that the strongest species will win out. . ." (M39). The animalistic Count gets on famously with his son-in-law Dr. Zawacki. Zawacki refuses to attend church, blasphemes against God, Jesus, the Apostles. His "humanism" is a function of his materialism and naturalism: "He agreed with Darwin that man was descended from the ape, and he contended that humans were the only intelligent beings in the cosmos. There were no truths beyond man's comprehension" (M222). Naturalism is incompatible with Judaism because it is incompatible with religion as such. But it is also capable, in its Darwinian form, of development into a creed of antisemitism. The novel's pioneer in this direction is Alexander Zipkin, a vulgar medical student who seduces Clara Kaminer, the sensuous young second wife of Calman Jacoby. In what the poverty of language compels Singer to call Zipkin's mind, naturalism, humanism, and antisemitism are inseparable. Since his mental operations are representative of a good many of the emancipated young Jews both of Ezriel's generation and the one to follow, they merit full illustration:

The conversation turned to religion. Zipkin said straight out that he was an atheist. People spoke of God, but where was He? Had anyone seen Him? Each race worshipped a different idol. Man, as Darwin had proved, was descended from the apes. He was just another animal: *homo sapiens*. Zipkin began discussing the doctrines of Marx, Lassalle, and Lavrov. The Polish Jew, he said, . . . had outlived his role and become little more than a parasite. He wasn't productive, didn't speak the language of the country in which he lived, and sent his children to cheders. How long was the Jew going to wash himself in ritual baths and walk around in tzizis? (M291–92)

The implication of labeling Jews parasites, unspoken by Zipkin but soon articulated by Ezriel's sister Mirale and her progressive friends, is that they should be exterminated—what else does one do with parasites?

Now, one way in which modern novelists at odds with the Darwinist legacy have expressed their disageement is by asserting the freedom of individual character from the determinism of heredity and environment; and this is precisely what Singer does in his treatment of the varying fates of the children of the two patriarchs, Calman and Menachem Mendel. The most striking contrast is that afforded by Ezriel and his sister Mirale. Their departures from piety are distinguished from the outset because Ezriel's is impelled by love and Mirale's by hate. Ezriel espouses Jewish intellectual emancipation from religious fanaticism. The Jews are, to his view, intellectually backward, ignorant of magnetism, electricity, microscope, and telescope. "I must help these people emerge from darkness" (M35). As if to suggest the vast hopelessness of Ezriel's enlightening task, Singer shows him, as he says this, flinging a snowball at the darkening sky. Everywhere Ezriel hears the voices of progress, luring him away from Chasidism and toward enlightenment. He hears people like the convert Wallenberg and the progressive Aaron Lipman, whose unceasing theme is that the Jews must surrender their "Asiatic" or, more specifically, "Chinese" stationariness, and join the progressive civilization of Europe: " 'Mankind progresses,' " says Wallenberg, " 'but they remain as static as the Chinese behind the Great Wall' " (M37).

Gradually Ezriel's faith is undermined, and he marvels that light—which is, after all, an undoubted quality of matter—is not seen by the Jews, who remain woefully "blind to the obvious inconsistencies of their faith" (M57). He cannot comprehend how the Jews, immersed in squalor and battered by oppression, continue to believe in God's love for them. Out of intellectual scruple he separates himself from the communal joy of Chasidism and, despite the vehement objection of his father-in-law, Calman, leaves his wife and baby in order to study in Warsaw.

But Ezriel finds, as do all who follow this road in *The Manor* and *The Estate,* that the life of an intellectual is joyless, isolated, artificial, oppressive. It may offer a way out of the constricted, regulated life of orthodox Judaism: it does not offer freedom. On the contrary, Ezriel finds the secular spirituality which prevails in the "emancipated" world of intellectual Warsaw far more demanding and infinitely more bewildering than the spirituality of religion. Here, as in religious life, everything is guided by rules, but these are not written down and they vary according to time and place, lacking not only unity but any claim to divine authority.

How should he behave tomorrow at Justina Malewska's? Should he kiss her hand? Pay her a compliment? . . . What should he do if he were offered food? . . . How long should he stay? Should he extend his hand first?. . . Did he need a calling-card? . . . He must learn worldly manners, choose the right profession, and after all that he would still be nothing but a persecuted Jew. . . . How odd, that the future world was easier by far than this one. In it, there was one reckoning, God. Here one was forced to consider countless directors, inspectors, laws, regulations, rules of etiquette, form—a code far more complex than the Shulhan Aruk, the book containing the Jewish laws. (M195)

This secular *Shulhan Aruk,* this holy book of worldliness, Ezriel eventually discovers, can never be fathomed by those who were not brought up on it, and even its lifelong devotees can never be sure that they are not transgressing its rules.

Ezriel's great hope had been to achieve progress through education. But as his own education proceeds, he begins to doubt the fundamental assumptions—naturalistic and materialistic—of modern knowledge itself. "The entities which were said to constitute matter seemed to have almost magical properties." But suppose these assumptions were true—that would be even worse, for it would make a mockery of any ascription of value to that ethical idealism which knowledge was supposed to serve. "The various materialistic theories, and Darwinism in particular, had put almost all values in jeopardy: the soul, ethics, the family. Might was right every where. Man's ancient beliefs had been bartered for the telegraph." Ezriel finds that he has abandoned the old traditions for a regimen of "nothing but examinations and dread"; having declared his independence of God, he finds himself "dependent upon all kinds of bureaucrats"(M286). Ezriel senses that he has made a catastrophic error, but one which he is still incapable of either defining or rectifying.

Mirale has also gone in for world-bettering (the welfare of the Jews being for her much too parochial a concern). Her method is not medicine but revolution. Her father is disturbed that Mirale at age twenty-four spends her time not with husband and children but away from home in the physical and spiritual ambience of enlightened secularists, discussing Buckle, Mill, Czernishewski, women's rights, peasants, revolution. He asks her why one should resist evil if one denies the existence of God, of divine law and judgment. She answers with the self-sufficiency of the proud humanist: " 'Because one is a human being.' " But Menachem Mendel Babad recognizes no middle ground between holiness and animalism: ".'A human being! If one does not serve the Almighty, one is even less than an animal. Animals kill only for food; murderers enjoy killing' "(M250). Everything that we learn of Mirale's subsequent career confirms the accuracy of this warning against the blood-lust which lies at the core of secular idealism.

Ezriel too attends some of the radical gatherings which are his
sister's spiritual nourishment. But he is considered too "negative"
and "pessimistic." In fact, it is his residual Jewishness that makes
him suspect among these non-Jewish Jews pretending to be Russians, Poles, and citizens of the world. His Jewish identity expresses
itself in two ways. First, Ezriel adheres doggedly to the biblical
principle that human life is invaluable and that murder is therefore
an absolute wrong, a sin not subject to human discussion and ra-
tionalization. Moreover, using terrorism to reform society is like
summoning a butcher when a surgeon is needed. But Mirale and
the other budding terrorists, he sees, do not merely offer pragmatic
justifications for political murder; they love it for its own sake as
something which fills a void in their souls. Second, Ezriel insists
on pointing out that universalism is really the peculiarly Jewish
form of parochialism, and is taken up by Jewish leftists to conceal
from themselves the knowledge of the ultimate target of revolutions:
the Jews. Zipkin is furious with Ezriel for bringing up this unspeak-
ably parochial matter of the Jews: " 'Jews? Why bring up the Jewish
question?' 'Well, what will happen to the Jews? Are we to be destroyed because we don't have a peasantry?' " Zipkin's answer is,
in effect, yes. Ezriel relentlessly presses the question: " 'Does this
include your own father?' " " 'Yes,' " replies Zipkin, " 'my father,
along with the rest.' " Mirale, aware that her brother has forced his
antagonists to that dark and bloody crossroads where utopianism
and Judaism always collide, rebukes him and also endorses the
antisemitic murderousness of naturalist progressivism: "Mirale began to shout, 'Ezriel, you're getting too personal. Leave our parents
and the Jews out of it. Sit down, Zipkin. I agree with you. A parasite
is a parasite, even if he's your father' "(M328–29).
    More than anything else, it is the irresistible attraction to violence
of these Jewish leftists which leads Ezriel to rethink his assumptions
about the absolute superiority of progressive European culture to
stationary Jewish religion.

"Why are they all so bloodthirsty?" Ezriel wondered. They were Jewish
women, members of the race which had sworn to uphold the Ten Commandments. Mirale was only one generation removed from their father
and mother. Only a short time before, she had been reading their mother's
prayer book. . . . He recalled the winter day in Jampol when Mirale had
entered the study house to tell him that Calman Jacoby had come to meet

him. Now he spent his time cutting the dead apart, and Mirale plotted to kill the living.(M330)

Zipkin, asked by Ezriel to name the results of the thousands of years of political violence, can offer nothing better than the "progressiveness" of European culture: " 'Civilization. Our modern world, with all its virtues and faults' "(M331). He makes explicit what all Ezriel's experiences with modernity seem to suggest: that to cease being a traditional Jew in order to become a European is to embrace a misery and boredom which can only be assuaged by violence or lust.

Ezriel, revolted by physical violence, seeks other means to lighten the burden of that ennui and nervousness which seem endemic to the enlightened and educated. He falls in love with a convert, the widow Olga Bielikov. Too rational and enlightened for Judaism, she is a devotee of spiritualism, which she hopes will put her in touch with her dead husband. She is but one among many characters in the novel who lead Ezriel to the conclusion that "among the rationalists, one found the most irrational people"(E189). Nevertheless, he (like Calman's errant daughter Miriam Lieba) thinks of romantic love as expressing a far more profound psychology of human behavior than the Talmud's, and the prospect of an affair with Olga at once replaces boredom with expectation. Not even the comments on Gentile political violence express so contemptuous a view of European culture as Singer's account of what runs through Ezriel's mind at the outset of this sordid infidelity: " 'I am a doctor, I am carrying on an affair. What could be more European than that? I've gone pretty far since Jampol' "(M415).

The relation between lust and violence is axiomatic in Singer's work, and nowhere expressed more powerfully than in this novel. The chief exponent of Singer's oft-repeated view that the prohibitions against adultery and against murder are inextricably and organically linked is Ezriel's foil among his own generation, Jochanan, the rabbi of Marshinov and husband to Calman's youngest daughter, Tsipele. Calman had substituted her—when she was but eleven years old—as a future match for Jochanan when the romantically inclined (and novel-reading) Miriam Lieba refused to have him. Yet this marriage, contrary to all the expectations of enlightened readers as well as the requirements of modern, secular love, is—as Mary Ellmann points out[5]—the most nearly perfect in the book: "Tsipele

turned to go. Jochanan's eyes followed her. A child in a bonnet and
dress, and a mother too. It was all the same to her, and that's the
way it should be. . . . Jochanan was lost in meditation. Yes, she had
the soul of a saint, a pure body. Satan had no power over such
creatures. It was said of them they were conceived and born in
holiness. Jochanan experienced a powerful feeling of love for Tsipele, who although she lived in the lower world reached those
heights that were beyond all material laws"(M170).
    Jochanan is a foil to Ezriel in professional as well as married life.
Consulted by a young man suffering from sexual impotence, Ezriel
the psychiatrist prescribes hydropathy. For recommending "the
emancipated ritual bath," Ellmann comments acidly,[6] Ezriel asks
a forty-kopeck fee. But when Jochanan the rabbi is consulted by a
man whose daughter suffers from terrible stomach pains and who
has received conflicting medical opinion about the wisdom of sur-
gery, he refuses to accept money and instead gives the man his gold
watch—a wedding present from Calman—to pay for another opinion. More important, he gives the man—because he desperately
wants it—his "promise" that the daughter will recover. For how
can one avoid such compromises with worldly pride except by leaving the world altogether?
    Jochanan is one of the novel's earliest general critics of all those
Jews who escape from the yoke of Torah, whether to kill off un-
progressive classes or to pursue unsanctified loves. His Yom Kippur
sermon on a text from Isaiah—"But the wicked are like the troubled
sea when it cannot rest, whose waters cast up mire and dirt"—deals
with the enlightened Jews, who " 'always wage something—war or
love.' " At first the two enterprises may seem unconnected, even
antithetical. But in fact they are related genuses belonging to the
species idolatry. Jochanan articulates in traditional language the
antihumanistic insight which pervades the book: "Man is born to
serve. If he does not serve God, he serves man." The prohibition
against idolatry is at the root of everything. Those who don't believe
in the Creator admire only flesh and blood: human riches, human
beauty, human wisdom, human power. Belief exclusively in the
natural and the material leads inevitably to jealousy, which breeds
cruelty and conflict. " 'The love of the wicked is as destructive as
war. The wicked man wants to take what another possesses. He
looks on a woman as booty. Though at first he may treat her gently,
once he has satisfied his lust, he will torture her. The love of the

wicked is basically violent' "(E81–82). Calman, hearing this sermon, rightly thinks of the way in which his second wife Clara and her lover Zipkin work to destroy each other. The reader thinks of Ezriel and Olga, still more of Miriam and Lucian, in whom the link between lust and murder is first a mental obsession, then an actuality. When Lucian is asked by the young girl Kasia how he can intend to make love to her when he already has a wife, his response is that it is possible, in nature, to have two wives. Unfortunately—thanks, he says, to the Jews—nature has been thwarted and corrupted. " 'Yes, it's possible, but forbidden. In our times there's so much that is forbidden. Don't do this, don't do that. It's our legacy from the Jews' "(M219). Here the Gentile revolutionary sounds very much like the Jewish ones. Neither can accept the Jewish view that morality is a bridle and not a spur.

Clara, in her own way, also rejects this Jewish "negativism" which insists on limiting experience by artificial distinctions. For Clara, life is not defined by distinctions between right and wrong, but between experience and inexperience. She is a devotee of what in modern educational jargon is called "experiential learning." As she is being seduced by Zipkin, she thinks: "She'd had husbands, but no lovers. If she waited much longer, she might be denied that experience." The reader can only hope that death, with which she is as compulsively obsessed as Lucian, will prove a richer and more rewarding educational experience than life has turned out to be, especially in the area of what Jochanan calls sexual violence or lust. As she and Zipkin move toward their adulterous bed, everything around them is redolent of death: " 'The whole building is like a cemetery,' he said." " 'Sometimes I think the whole world is a cemetery,' Clara answered"(M293–94). Clara's son Sasha is the logical fruit of her womb and of Zipkin's tutoring. Having been schooled not in the *Ethics of the Fathers* but in "manners," he shames his father, Calman, by aping the ways of army officers and dandies. His mother's sexual experiments were confined to Jews, whereas he branches out to the wives of army officers; but the springs of action are the same: "The main thing was not to pass up any opportunity"(E86).

Ezriel's children, on the other hand, prove as rebellious to him as he had been to his father. But their rebelliousness takes different (if not exactly antithetical) forms. Neither Joziek nor his sister Zina is particularly attracted to their father's ideal of improvement through enlightenment. But they, like him, choose to live outside the boundaries of piety, the yoke of the Torah.

Zina is very much, like her aunt Mirale (now in exile in Siberia), the garden-variety Jewish leftist. The Socialist antisemitism of her aunt is more likely to be expressed by her as anti-Zionism, a fury toward "this new nationalism of the vicious Jewish capitalists"(E327). But she too believes in the redemptive power of violence and revolution. Indeed, Ezriel's discovery of her gun and cartridges is a decisive moment in his own spiritual development. "It was the first time in Ezriel's life that he had touched such an instrument of destruction, and its weight astounded him. He didn't know how to handle it. . . ." Ezriel's revulsion from the weapon is inseparable from his anger towards himself for having raised non-Jewish children. "He had taught her everything, except Judaism. . . . Ezriel reminded himself of a saying in *The Best of Pearls:* 'The children are the secrets in the hearts of their parents' "(E231–32).

That his own daughter should be soiled by the Gentile religion of violence seems to Ezriel a revelation of the true character of Jewish identity, which is epitomized by powerlessness. "Jewish suffering had produced a spiritually superior type. For two thousand years the Jew had not been in power and had not carried a sword"(E246). But Ezriel is not permitted to rest in this conclusion prompted by his daughter's treachery, for the experience of his other child shows him that it is far too comfortable and complacent, and that the Jews are now put to a hard choice between the supposed virtue of powerlessness and their survival as a people.

The significant entry into the novel of Ezriel's son Joziek comes when he announces to his father: " 'I'm going to Palestine.' " Although—or because—he attends a "modern" school, Joziek has suffered from antisemitism. He recounts the incident which has at last brought him to his decision:

"Someone poured water into my cap. I came home without it, without my honor too. Papa, I can't stand it any more! I'd rather die."
"Well, we've lived like this for two thousand years."
"That's long enough. A man who can't speak up when his cap is being filled with water is no man."

Once again, but in very different circumstances from those which obtained in his sister's circle of parlor revolutionaries, Ezriel is brought to face the question of force. He rebukes his son for thinking he will escape from violence in Palestine, where " 'a Turk might hit you, or an Arab.' " But Joziek replies confidently that there, in his own land, he would be able to strike back. For him as for his father, this question of violence has been decisive, but in a way surprising to Ezriel. His son rejects the promises of enlightenment and assimilation because they invite him to share the beliefs and manners of those who wallow in the filth of antisemitism: " 'I can't take on the beliefs of those who beat me' "(E57–60). When we next hear of Joziek, he is called Uri Joseph. He is living in Palestine and his photograph shows him on a horse, carrying a rifle for self-defense.

Since the horse and the gun were (as we noted at the beginning of this chapter) in the eyes of the Eastern European Jew the peculiar accoutrements of the Gentile, it might seem that Zionism is here being depicted as (what the orthodox often alleged it was) nothing but another form of assimilation. If this were so, then the hope for reintegration of that Jewish life which we have watched disintegrating in Poland would prove as illusory in the Land of Israel as in America (to which Zipkin and Clara move). But Singer does not depict Zionism as yet another dead-end. Rather, he suggests that Zionism represents the one way in which the Jews can retain their traditional culture in an increasingly secular world. "Joziek was not religious but he had remained a Jew. Now he even wrote in Hebrew and signed his letters Uri Joseph. He had married a Jewish girl. His children would be educated in Hebrew schools"(E249). As the most articulate contemporary expositor of Zionism has written: "A land and a language! They are the ground beneath a people's feet and the air it breathes in and out. With them all things are possible, for each is an inexhaustible treasure. . . ."[7]

For Ezriel, Zionism—unbeknownst, perhaps, to its most ardent advocates—is a manifestation of the continuing vitality of Judaism and of the chosenness of the Jewish People. "In the passage of two thousand years, hundreds of nations had become assimilated into other cultures. But the Jews still struggled to return to the land of their ancestors. This fact alone proved that the Old Testament contained divine truths"(E246–47). Ezriel, like many another Zionist, does not return to the homeland himself. His Zionism is a return to the Jewish people before it is a return to the Land. As is the case with nearly all of Singer's penitents, Ezriel's return is hedged about with doubts and hesitation. Yet the dominant movement of the last segment of *The Estate* is defined by Ezriel's repudiation of Enlightenment for Chasidism and of Europe for Palestine. The Chasidim become the living embodiment of the virtues of standing still—"In their Houses of Worship, it is always the beginning"—and of contempt for ideas of progress and perpetual movement. Only among these people of whom the Enlightenment had taught him to be ashamed can Ezriel find joy. Among the followers of Rabbi Jochanan,

eyes shone, faces glowed. . . . What he saw here was completely contrary to the textbooks. According to the sociologists, poverty was the cause not only of sickness but of crime. But these Jews were a living denial of all these theories. . . . This was. . . an assemblage of paupers, less secure than the peasantry and the proletariat. They had been driven out of Russia, were the victims of pogroms; writers had vilified them, called them parasites; anti-Semites had manufactured false accusations against them. But instead of becoming degenerate, sinking into melancholy, drunkenness, immorality—they celebrated, recited the Psalms, rejoiced with happiness that could only come from the soul. No one here was in despair over the pogroms, as were the Jewish intelligentsia all over Russia. They placed their faith in God, not in man, evolution, or revolution.(E346)

Ezriel's passionate admiration for a faith he cannot share goes hand in hand with a conviction (fully borne out by events even *before* 1939)[8] that the Jews had no future in Poland, which considered them foreigners even after an eight-hundred-year sojourn in that land. Indeed, Jewish existence is withering away everywhere in the Diaspora, from internal as well as external causes. " 'We remain alien, always the object of mockery and derision. Nothing has changed. Conditions are as bad today as they were a thousand years ago. Even worse: in those days, there was no "enlightenment." In those days, at least, Jews kept their faith. . .' "(E359). The only answer to Ezriel's unsatisfied spiritual aspirations as to his instinctive desire to live rather than to die, is the hope of Zion. In his last utterance of the book, he writes to Zadok that he has decided to go to Palestine because "Palestine is for me the symbol of the return to my roots, the source of the ancient truths that for thousands of years people have tried to alter, emasculate, or drown in dogma"(E364). If the Jews of the Diaspora have been truly a dispersed rather than a dismembered people,[9] then they must have had through the millennia, and they still do have, a spiritual and a physical center.

CHAPTER 7

Enemies, A Love Story

As I prophesied, there was a noise, and behold a commotion, and the bones came together, bone to its bone. And I beheld, and, lo, there were sinews upon them, and flesh came up, and skin covered them above; but there was no breath in them.

—Ezekiel, 37:7–8

MANY of Singer's short fictions, most notably "Gimpel the Fool," treat the world of East European Jewry as if the Holocaust had never occurred, "as if," in the words of one critic, "it were still radiantly alive: the Hasidim still dancing, the rabbis still pondering, the children still studying . . . as if it had not all ended in ashes and death."[1] But novels such as *The Manor, The Estate,* and *The Family Moskat* deliberately view the Jews as prospective victims of the Holocaust, whose every opinion, preference, and action takes its special coloring from our awareness of the impending fate of all European Jewry. *Enemies* treats the survivors of the Holocaust as if they were now the central bearers of Jewish fate, and as if the definition and resolution of the ultimate questions of philosophy, politics, and religion can never again be made without reference to their experience.

Singer assumes that there is no such thing as the Holocaust experience *per se* apart from the experiences of a host of individual survivors, and therefore no possibility of arriving at general assertions about the ultimate meaning of the Holocaust that are not qualified by our awareness of the peculiarities of the victims. Neither is it possible to speak about the effects of the Holocaust even on an individual survivor without knowing that person's prior history. He warns in his prefatory note that his "characters are not only Nazi victims but victims of their own personalities and fates. If they fit into the general picture, it is because the exception is rooted in the rule. As a matter of fact, in literature the exception *is* the rule." By way of illustrating his meaning, Singer often in the novel reminds us that his hero Herman Broder "had been a victim long before Hitler's day" (121), and that his suicidal hedonism and fatalism had been confirmed, but not caused, by Hitler.

Enemies explores the relationship between survivors of the Holocaust living in the United States and their own experience during the Second World War. All four major characters as well as most of the minor ones are survivors, although their experiences of horror differed in kind and degree. Herman Broder's family had been murdered by the Germans, but he had survived because a Polish servant of his father's had hidden him (at great risk to herself) in a hayloft in her native village. After the war Herman had married this Gentile woman in a civil ceremony—"it seemed senseless to burden her with a religion that he himself no longer observed"—and taken her to live in Brooklyn, which is where we find them as the novel opens. Yadwiga is utterly devoted to Herman, kind, generous, and desirous of acquiring Jewish ways and the Jewish religion. But Yadwiga is for Herman an absurd anomaly in an evil world: "Yadwiga's sheer goodness bored him" (23). Blessed with one of the rare lights that shone in the Gentile world during the Holocaust, Herman prefers to believe in the general darkness as the ultimate reality. His real love, and also his mistress, is a Jewish survivor named Masha, who had endured years in the ghetto and concentration camps. They had met and fallen in love while still in Germany after the war. It is for Masha's sake that Herman deceives Yadwiga by telling her that he works as a book salesman and must therefore be frequently away from home. Herman's desire to immerse himself forever in the darkness of the Holocaust can be amply satisfied by the nervous, hysterical, and bitter Masha.

Yadwiga represents the claims of the past upon Herman, Masha the claims of the present and of his own sensual inclination. But there is yet a third claim upon Herman in the form of his first wife Tamara. Long presumed dead, she now "rises from the dead" after having wandered through Russia and suffered terribly in Soviet camps as well as Nazi ones during the war years. Not resurrected, however, are the two children of Tamara and Herman, Yocheved and David. Herman's first marriage had been dismal even before the catastrophe. Tamara had been one of those numerous Singer women who prefer ideologies and slogans to life and feeling. First a Communist, then a Zionist, always a feminist, she had been "constantly celebrating, protesting, signing petitions, and raising funds for all kinds of party purposes." Later, in reaction to the Nazis and their Polish antisemitic followers, she had turned to religion. But, when we meet her, the Holocaust has burned away much of the fret and fume of her former existence. Like Yadwiga, she represents a claim of the past on Herman, and one which is enforced by the memory of their dead children, toward whom Herman has more than the usual "survivors' guilt" because he had often denied their existence in his desire to live up to the role of the bachelor that he was not.

What little story the novel has consists of Herman's attempts to resolve the competing claims of the three women, two his wives and the third eager to become one. The drama is played out in several of the boroughs of New York City, which for the survivors is virtually coextensive with "America." We must remember that Singer had been living in this country since 1935, so that by the time of the publication of *Enemies* in Yiddish (1966) he had lived in New York for as long as he had lived in Poland. He writes of the American setting (especially of distinctly "Jewish" areas like Coney Island or the Catskills) with considerable authority and circumstantial detail.

He writes of it, too, with a good deal of ill-concealed distaste, despite his strong political attachment to what American represents, his deep dislike of the anti-American cabal of Communist nations, and his corrosive contempt for the American intellectual admirers of communism. Although the historical and social reality is barely glanced at, Singer writes in full awareness of the fact that, during the Holocaust, the American Jewish community, the largest and most powerful (or, to be scrupulously accurate, least powerless) Jewish community in the world, had done very little to save the Jews of Europe. During the war, American policy toward rescuing Jews from Europe might have become the occasion of a tragic conflict of loyalties for the American Jews. Yehuda Bauer has succinctly described that policy as follows: "Every humanitarian consideration was dropped, and the slogan 'rescue through victory' became the statement of official policy. This policy did not take into account that few Jews would remain to be rescued after victory."[2] But the conflict never occurred: the Jews of Europe were left to be murdered, and their American brethren, with notable exceptions, either took refuge in "common-sensical" incredulity about what was hap-

pening or callously ignored the Holocaust even though they credited
it. This is the background against which we must view Herman
Broder's unease in American Jewish society.

Although Herman is besieged by fantasies of the Nazis invading
and occupying New York, he finds himself, whenever he risks the
danger of social life, among people whose life and consciousness
had never been touched in the slightest by the Holocaust. "Half of
his people had been tortured and murdered, and the other half
were giving parties" (213–14). At one such party in a Jewish resort,
the spectacle of Jewish life untouched by the Holocaust fills Herman
with revulsion and a metaphysical disgust with worldly existence
itself:

> The Yiddish poet gave a speech, lauding Stalin, and recited proletarian
> poetry. An actress did impersonations of celebrities. . . .An actor . . . told
> bawdy jokes about a betrayed husband, whose wife had hidden a Cossack
> under her bed, and about a rabbi who had come to preach to a loose woman
> and had left her house with his fly open. . . ."Why is it all so painful to
> me?" Herman asked himself. The vulgarity in this casino denied the sense
> of creation. It shamed the agony of the holocaust. (120–21)

Had the Jews who survived the Holocaust survived only for this?

The failure of American Jewry to establish its claim as the inheritor
of Jewish collective existence after the destruction of the historic
centers of Jewish population and culture in Europe is felt throughout
the book. Yadwiga, a Gentile who asks her neighbors in Coney
Island to instruct her in Judaism and "Jewishness," comes away
with the impression that the possession of modern electrical appli-
ances and a substantial life-insurance policy is as necessary a part
of Judaism as observing the sabbath and kashrut. The one prominent
rabbi in the book is Herman's employer, Rabbi Lampert, whose
antics with Masha late in the story give him a resemblance to the
rabbinical scoundrel in the story told by the actor at the party.
Lampert, more a businessman than a spiritual leader, employs
Herman, a former Talmudist, to write his sermons and articles.

But it is not only the vulgarity and materialism of American Jewish
life which make America seem alien and inhospitable to the Holocaust survivor attached to his experience. The very experience is
inconceivable to those who did not endure it. Tamara can hardly
credit her own story, much less convey it to others. " 'What happened to me can never be fully told. The truth is, I don't really

know myself. So much happened that I sometimes imagine nothing happened.' " It is, she repeatedly tells her curious husband—and she is referring to the exploits of Stalin as well as Hitler—futile to try to relate what is "beyond belief " (73).

Yet once Singer has taken account of those characteristics both of the Holocaust and of American Jewish life which tend to separate the survivors from their experience, he makes it clear that the Holocaust will affect the Jews more, rather than less, with the passage of time. Shifrah Puah, Masha's mother, always wears black and is immersed in the Holocaust even though she now lives in New York. "She continued to live in spirit with those who had been gassed and tortured." She reads the Yiddish newspapers only for accounts of survivors and uses all the money she can spare from food to buy books about the death camps. "Other refugees used to say that with time one forgets, but neither Shifrah Puah nor Masha would ever forget. On the contrary, the further removed they were from the holocaust, the closer it seemed to become" (43).

For those who went through it, the Holocaust has imposed itself as the paradigm of all history. No matter where or when you exist in the aftermath of the Holocaust, you exist in a new epoch, whose essential conditions are defined by what happened in the Holocaust itself. " 'We came out of Gehenna,' says Shifrah Puah, 'but Gehenna followed us to America' " (184). In the nights which are made endless by his insomnia, Herman wages an endless war against the Nazis. In Masha's every dream, she is besieged by Germans who are dragging, beating, and chasing her. Nor is the eternal presentness of this nightmare past entirely something imposed from without. Tamara treasures the German bullet in her side as her "best souvenir," which keeps alive her memory of home, parents, children—and what happened to them (190). She and her uncle Reb Abraham Nissen do not ever want to forget what they went through. They value their suffering, and Nissen even insists that Jews should observe an eternal mourning: " 'The entire people should squat on low stools and read from the Book of Job' " (239).

This is not simply a matter of the aftereffects of the Holocaust lingering on to plague the survivors. Rather, it is a terrifying recognition that the Holocaust revealed the essential character of history. For Herman, the Holocaust has collapsed distinctions of time and made out of the murderous events of history its true and enduring pattern: "Cain continues to murder Abel. Nebuchadnezzar is still slaughtering the sons of Zedekiah. . . .The pogrom in Kesheniev never ceases. Jews are forever being burned in Auschwitz" (30). The Holocaust has also consumed and determined the future: " 'Everything has already happened,' Herman thought. 'The creation, the flood, Sodom, the giving of the Torah, the Hitler holocaust.' Like the lean cows of Pharaoh's dream, the present had swallowed eternity, leaving no trace" (156). As the creation had been undone by the flood, so the Holocaust has undone the covenant. Moreover, the destruction which befell Sodom as a city all of whose inhabitants had become equally guilty, was universalized by the Holocaust.

If the Holocaust presents itself to Herman as a reversal of nineteenth-century attempts to make History into a God (when in fact it is the Devil), Masha expresses her bitterness by a revulsion against Nature (that other nineteenth-century candidate for godhead). " 'It can happen again. Slaughtering Jews is part of nature. Jews must be slaughtered—that's what God wants' " (37). She has no patience with Herman's vegetarianism because it denies the underlying principle of the whole system of nature: " 'God himself eats meat— human flesh' " (33). Herman too is astonished at the naiveté of Plato in asserting that it is "against nature" that a good man should be hurt by a bad one. "Was this really so? Was it against nature that the Nazis should have murdered millions of Jews?" (217).

These reactions, Singer knows, will appear "excessive" only to those too shallow to recognize that our era has witnessed events of biblical enormity. The Holocaust—by which is meant specifically the Nazis' systematic destruction of every Jew for the crime of having been born—is overwhelming not only in the magnitude of its destruction but in the uniqueness of its evil. That 5.8 million Jews, approximately one-third of the Jewish world population, should have been done to death with utmost cruelty; that the spiritual and biological centers of world Jewry should have been decimated; that the nations among whom the Jews of Europe lived should have done little to save them and much to doom them; all this would in itself be appalling enough to convince the Jewish survivors that not just a third of their people but a third of their own souls now lay in the grave. But the Germans had murdered millions of other people, too—among them Russians, Poles, Gypsies. The uniqueness of the "final solution" was that only in this instance, only with the Jews, did the Germans decide that they were dealing with nonhumans, every single one of whom must be killed only because he was born and for no other crime. Large segments of the Polish and Russian nations had to be eliminated so that the rest could be made into a slave nation serving Aryans; but not every Pole and Russian, not even every Gypsy, was under sentence of death.[3] The Jews had become the first (though not necessarily the last) victims of genocide.

Singer knows, as do his major characters, that the Jewish people has in the recent past gone through a crisis unprecedented in its history. Neither he nor they can be certain that the crisis is over; and they feel too close to the terrible event to be sure that anything of permanent value has survived the storm or can be built in its wake. Gershom Scholem, one of the greatest of modern Jewish thinkers, has written that "it is not surprising that there are as yet no signs of a reaction, of one kind or another, to the profound shock of the Holocaust. Such a reaction, when it comes, could be either deadly or productive."[4]

Those who went to Israel after the war as a matter of choice (rather than necessity) believed in the possibility, at least, of a productive reaction, a renewal of Jewish collective life in the ancient homeland now that the Diaspora had been destroyed. Those who chose America were more likely to have been thinking of individual than collective survival and renewal, yet we ought not to rule out the possibility that for some of them too America offered the possibility of a collective Jewish renewal, a Bene Brak or Yavneh which would preserve Jewish life after its historic centers had been destroyed. In *Enemies*, however, we hear nothing of this from Herman or his several women and their relatives. They are more likely to respond to the "deadly" metaphysical implications of the Holocaust, which are summed up by Herman: "Religions lied. Philosophy was bankrupt from the beginning. The idle promises of progress were no more than a spit in the face of the martyrs of all generations" (30).

Religion, philosophy, and political idealism have all been called into question by the Holocaust. Political philosophies built on the belief in progress stink in Herman's nostrils. He is revolted by an article in a Yiddish paper which looks forward to the establishment of a social system based on perfect equality and justice to "cure the sickness of the world." Still the desire to cure what is in its nature incurable! Still the mindless optimism which is convinced that par-

tial evil ultimately subserves the cause of universal good! Herman's
disbelief in progress is carried a step further by Masha's ex-husband,
Leon Tortshiner. He contends that " 'the human species is getting
worse, not better. I believe . . . in an evolution in reverse. The last
man on earth will be both a criminal and a madman' " (163). Nevertheless, among many of the Jews the fascination with socialist and
revolutionary political movements continues unabated, in spite of
the fact that Hitler's National Socialism was the most thoroughgoing
revolution the world had ever known. No matter how gruesome are
Tamara's accounts of the bestialities in Stalin's slave-labor camps,
many Jews continue to be, as Herman says, "hypnotized" by Communism. "In the name of Lenin and Stalin, Communists had tortured elderly teachers, and annihilated whole villages in China and
Korea in the name of 'cultural' revolution. . . . In Moscow they had
liquidated all the Jewish writers. Yet Jewish Communists in New
York, Paris, and Buenos Aires praised the murderers and reviled
yesterday's leaders" (248).

Herman understands the lunatic persistence among Jews of
utopianism for what it is: a modern form of the old idolatry outlawed
by Judaism. He tells Masha: " 'The Gentile makes gods of stone
and we of theories' " (110). Herman, a learned man, knows that
true Jewish universalism means that the God of the Jews is the God
of all mankind, not that the idols of mankind must be the gods of
the Jews. Yet the very cataclysm which has made the "belief" in
mankind an impossibility for him has also called into doubt every
other attempt to impose order and meaning on the universe. "Truth?
Not in this jungle, this saucer of earth perched over hot lava. God?
Whose God? The Jews'? Pharaoh's?" (248).

The recurrent conflict between faith and doubt is as much a drama
of this novel as the competition among his three women for the
possession of Herman Broder. Some of the minor characters, like
Masha's mother and Tamara's uncle and aunt, have remained observant and pious. Virtually all the major figures are rent with
bitterness, and lurch in fits and starts sometimes in the direction
of paradoxical faith, sometimes in the direction of uneasy (rather
than smug) denial. Masha, whose corrosive bitterness foretells her
suicide from the novel's outset, is not an atheist, but something
more terrifying. She believes that God was deeply implicated in
the Holocaust, because "the true God" hates the Jews, whereas
they have invented an idol who is alleged to have loved and chosen

them. She cannot live without God, nor with Him. Hitler, she
insists, executed God's purposes. "When she talked of German
atrocities, she would run to the mezuzah and spit on it" (43). If the
God invented by the Jews intended to improve his people by sub-
jecting them to the Holocaust, then certainly he failed, for the
religious Jews faithful to him had been practically wiped out, whereas the worldly Jews who managed to escape had learned exactly
nothing from the terror and slaughter.

Tamara, herself resurrected from the dead, believes in souls and
in their resurrection. She admires those, like her pious aunt and
uncle, who can go through hell yet remain healthy and whole because they resign themselves to God's will. But although she admires the moral results of belief, she herself cannot believe. She
believes in a soul, but not in its creator. Her loss of her children,
and the suffering she witnessed and endured in the camps convinced
her that " 'the merciful God in whom we believed does not
exist' "(81). But she also saw how, under extreme conditions, most
people will descend below the human status but a few will rise
above it; and these rare exceptions are enough to vindicate her
belief in the possibility of sustaining a humane existence in this
world. She saw not only adults but children achieve a beauty and
serenity of existence previously unknown to her. Some of these
children, going to their death like saints, convinced her that " 'souls
exist; it's God who doesn't' "(83).

Herman, the central character, oscillates wildly between blasphemous vilification of the "Almighty sadist" who has expressed his
unrivaled ingenuity in evil by creating Hitler and Stalin, and a
desire to forsake worldly existence altogether in favor of dedication
to Torah. He, like Tamara, respects the moral power of belief, or
at least the moral inutility of disbelief. Why, he keeps asking himself, is so much of Western civilization in its secular, modern guise
coextensive with murder and fornication? His answer is that once
the barriers imposed by religion are down, anything is possible.
This is especially true for the Jews, who are capable of every abomination once they are released from the yoke of the Torah.

If a Jew departed in so much as one step from the Shulchan Aruch, he
found himself spiritually in the sphere of everything base—Fascism,
Bolshevism, murder, adultery, drunkenness. . . . Who and what could
have controlled the Jewish members of the GPU, the Capos, the thieves,

speculators, informers? What could save him, Herman, from sinking even deeper into the mire in which he was caught? Not philosophy, not Berkeley, Hume, Spinoza, not Leibnitz, Hegel, Schopenhauer, Nietzsche, or Husserl. They all preached some sort of morality but it did not have the power to help withstand temptation. One could be a Spinozaist and a Nazi; one could be versed in Hegel's phenomenology and be a Stalinist; one could believe in monads, in the *Zeitgeist,* in blind will, in European culture, and still commit atrocities.(170).

This passionate indictment of the deep-seated corruption of the Western secular civilization which had tempted so many Jews away from Judaism states, in effect, that in morals as in physics the stream cannot rise higher than its source. Moral philosophies invented by men can never raise men above themselves; only a moral teaching revealed from above can do that. Herman thus recognizes with clarity that he can only escape from the meaningless pursuit of pleasure in which he and Masha are engaged by turning to God. "And to what faith could he repair? Not to a faith which had, in the name of God, organized inquisitions, crusades, bloody wars. There was only one escape for him: to go back to the Torah, the Gemara, the Jewish books." Nothing can protect one from infection by the moral quagmire that exists outside the grounds of the Torah. Sensing the futility of his endless deceptions and feeling that "he was suffocating without God and the Torah," Herman vows to change his life. Insisting that only two choices are available to Jews, he tells the astonished Yadwiga that he will never again violate the Sabbath because " 'if we don't want to become like the Nazis, we must be Jews' "(170–71).

Determined to repent, as hundreds of generations of Jews had done before him, Herman plans to leave his job with the rabbi (for how can true Judaism survive working for a rabbi?) and to leave Masha, who is too enmeshed in worldliness ever to contemplate repentance. Like that of so many other characters in Singer's fiction, Herman's contemplated return to Judaism is a kind of homecoming to the Jewish people as they are embodied in the memory of his ancestors. "He sat over his Gemara, staring at the letters, at the words. These writings were home. On these pages dwelt his parents, his grandparents, all his ancestors"(172).

But Herman's strength of intellect is not matched by strength of will. Not long after he resolves to become a good Jew, he falls away from the ideal and lapses into marriage (by means of a civil cere-

mony, to boot) with Masha, thus adding yet a third wife to the two
who represent his obligations to the past. Singer makes it clear that
it is a recurrent rather than a unique experience for Herman to
recognize the basis of his best, his true self, only to lapse back into
his ordinary self. Each time he is satiated with the empty materialism of worldly existence he takes down his volumes of the *Shulchan Aruch* and the Gemara, and then, a week or two later, he
finds himself staring at the bookcase "and at the volumes of the
Gemara which again stood neglected and dusty"(176). Again and
again, Herman's conversion proves abortive and his resolution
comes to nothing. "How many times had he made such resolutions!
How many times had he tried to spit in the face of worldliness, and
each time been tricked away"(213).

Why is it that Herman's conversion, his penitent return to Judaism, is impermanent? Both the antecedents and the process of
his conversion may be found in Singer's Eastern European Jews as
well. But when Yasha Mazur returns to Judaism, or Ezriel Babad
to the Jewish people, there is no question of backsliding. The dif-
ference is that Yasha and Ezriel lived in a world where Jews still
had a culture and a language and an inner world of their own, one
which could sustain waverers. American Jewry lacks such a world
and a culture, and therefore the medium which might support so
unsteady a character as Herman Broder. His spiritual aspirations
die for want of a nourishing atmosphere. Although he passes most
of his time among Jews and makes his living by ghostwriting sermons
and essays for a rabbi, Herman does not live in a Jewish world.
"The rabbi was selling God as Terah sold idols. . . . Modern Judaism
had one aim: to ape the Gentile"(19). Even Yiddish, though still
spoken by many of the characters, has lost its stature as a kind of
substitute for nationhood, and become the butt of cruel jokes. Tamara fears to leave her uncle's bookstore unlocked not because of
thieves but because "some Yiddish author might break in at night
and put in some more books"(261).

The single shared experience which might creatively shape the
inner life and direct the actions of a substantial group of American
Jews as we see them in this novel is the Holocaust. But does it?
We have already seen how, on the metaphysical level, the survivors
fall far short of that "productive" response to their crisis of which
Scholem speaks. But even the most elemental, physical response
to the Holocaust also proves beyond the capacities of the generality

of survivors we meet in Singer's America. The Germans had set out
to inflict death on the whole Jewish people, and had succeeded in
decimating European Jewry and reducing the world Jewish population by a third. As a result the very future of the Jewish people
is at stake.

To the prospect of extinction the natural, indeed the specifically
Jewish response as formulated in the Bible itself, would be: "I shall
not die, but live." It would be to produce children, to perpetuate
oneself and one's people. The philosopher Emil Fackenheim has
written that, after Auschwitz, "Jews are forbidden to hand Hitler
posthumous victories. They are commanded to survive as Jews, lest
the Jewish people perish. . . . A Jew may not respond to Hitler's
attempt to destroy Judaism by himself cooperating in its destruction.
In ancient times, the unthinkable Jewish sin was idolatry. Today,
it is to respond to Hitler by doing his work."[5] Yet this is precisely
what Singer's hero, in his despair, contemplates doing. Herman
returns obsessively, compulsively, and destructively to the subject
of child-bearing. We learn at the outset of the novel that Herman
took great care not to make Yadwiga pregnant because "in a world
in which one's children could be dragged away from their mother
and shot, one had no right to have more children"(7). Much later
in the novel we learn that "he didn't want to admit it, but of all his
fears, the greatest was his fear of again becoming a father"(149).

The children who are most alive in the story itself and in the
imagination of Herman and Tamara are little Yocheved and David,
both long dead, murdered by the Germans. Herman is burdened
with guilt for his neglect of them when they were alive, and it is
on their account that Tamara too opposes bringing any more Jewish
children into the world. " 'What for? So that the Gentiles will have
someone to burn?' "(101). The nightly visits she receives from these
children convince her either that they are somewhere alive or—
more probable—that she is herself dead: " 'A feeling remains: that
they exist somewhere and want to be in contact with me' "(137).
Herman, whose own inclination to believe in resurrection has been
greatly strengthened by Tamara's return from the dead, encourages
and partly shares her belief that the children do visit her. That
incredulity and worldliness which are the bane of Herman's existence in Jewish America and prevent him from believing in the
future are not permitted to penetrate the sanctuary of Holocaust

memory. " 'I believe you,' " he assures Tamara. " 'Those who doubt everything are also capable of believing everything' "(136).

But this willed belief in resurrection is the one act of defiance of empirical reality of which Herman is still capable; in every other respect it has overwhelmed him. This, ultimately, is why he cannot survive the Holocaust. He has cut himself off from every conceivable Jewish community because he knows that Jewish existence in the Diaspora has itself been a defiance of history, a willed indifference to empirical actuality and the convergence of probabilities (according to which the Jews should long ago have disappeared) made possible by an unreasoning faith in divine justice and the messianic hope. Early in the book Herman sees in the Botanical Gardens in Prospect Park a natural image of Jewish existence in Exile:

They stopped at the Botanical Gardens to look at the flowers, palms, cactuses, the innumerable plants grown in the synthetic climate of hothouses. The thought occurred to Herman that Jewry was a hothouse growth—it was kept thriving in an alien environment nourished by the belief in a Messiah, the hope of justice to come, the promises of the Bible—the Book that had hypnotized them forever.(52)

Hothouse growths, Herman recognizes, can be beautiful. Yet he believes that although the refusal to accept empirical reality as ultimate truth had sustained the Jews' life-giving belief in Messianic redemption, it had also been a contributing factor to their destruction at the hands of the Nazis.

In any case, Herman lacks not only the hothouse atmosphere required to keep Jewry alive in the Diaspora, but also that belief in a divinely imposed destiny which would give meaning to the struggle and suffering. No secular literature, "no matter how well written," can move him as the Bible moves him, or seem so immediate to all his moods. He can even understand his own predicament best in the terms laid down long ago by the Bible: "He was deceiving not only Abimelech but Sarah and Hagar as well." But without belief in the God who had imposed their unique destiny on the Jews, Herman cannot see why Jewish existence should be perpetuated. "Herman had not sealed a covenant with God and had no use for Him. He didn't want to have his seed multiply like the sands by the sea." Once he recognizes that his entire life is permeated by fraud and deception—"the sermons he had written for Rabbi Lampert, the books he sold to rabbis and yeshiva boys, his acceptance of Yadwiga's conversion to Judaism, and Tamara's favors"—nothin remains to him but a spiritually inconclusive petering out(248).

Indeed, his end is not only inconclusive but amorphous. The hope which had flickered for him and Masha (the one woman crucial to Herman's existence) turns to ashes in the mouth. Her pregnancy turns out to be imagined, her oaths about relations with her first husband prove to be lies. When she wants to stay with her dying mother until the end, Herman, disavowing all moral obligation because " 'we're not Jews any more' "(274), leaves Masha and the world of the novel as well. In the brief epilogue we learn of her suicide and of Herman's disappearance or death or—as Tamara believes—commitment to lifelong reenactment of the Holocaust reality by hiding somewhere in an American version of the Polish hayloft. Tamara, though she receives a rabbinical dispensation which would allow her to marry again, says that she would only consider doing so " 'in the next world—to Herman' "(280). Neither of Herman's surviving wives, in fact, will be troubled by the male principle. Tamara takes into her household Yadwiga and her baby— a daughter named Masha.

It is fitting that the book should end with the birth of Yadwiga's child after Herman himself has disappeared. Masha and Yadwiga had always wanted to have a child by the unwilling Herman, the former because she sought a means by which permanently to attach Herman to herself, the latter because she had accepted the moral imperative to preserve the Jewish people. The life-wisdom of this simple peasant had enabled her to see what was quite beyond the grasp of Jewish intellectualism and to declare: " 'I'm going to become Jewish. I want to have a Jewish child' "(149). Only Yadwiga the non-Jew is capable of recognizing that the preservation of the Jewish people after Auschwitz has not merely a Jewish but a universal human significance as an affirmation that no member of the family of nations shall be removed from the world to satisfy the blood-lust of another member. This simple yet profound recognition makes her unique among the characters of the novel and makes the birth of her daughter on "the night before Shevuot"(279) the single sign of hope that the plague of death will not spread from Europe to America.

CHAPTER 8

Shosha

Sing into the valley of bony words/rise up, letter by letter,/I love you, dead
world of my youth,/I command you, rise up, let your joy revive,/come
close, letter by letter, warm, pulsing,/meaning nothing,/ but dancing towards the world, blotting out the clouds like bright birds.

—Jacob Glatstein
(translated by Ruth Whitman)

ALTHOUGH it was originally published in Yiddish in the *Forward* in 1974 as *Soul Expeditions, Shosha* struck many of Singer's English readers as a fictionalized version of the autobiographical *A Young Man in Search of Love,* when both books
appeared almost simultaneously in 1978. *Shosha* is the only one of
Singer's novels published in English that is written in the first
person,[1] and it makes many explicit references to widely known
facts of his life, from his home address to his early difficulties as a
Yiddish writer to his conversion to vegetarianism. Those aspects of
his own experience and ideas which in previous novels were widely
distributed among his characters are here in a sense gathered back
to their source. Whether this turning in upon himself is a cause or
an effect of a diminished creative energy which this novel exhibits
is a question which only his future work can answer. *Shosha* is
better suited to satisfying the curiosities of readers about Singer's
character and personality than to answering the great questions to
which even this novel's characters still address themselves: *"What
can one do? How is one to live?"* (185).

Shosha, like *The Family Moskat,* is set in Poland between the
two World Wars. The inevitability of the Holocaust and the utter
powerlessness of the Jews in the face both of Polish antisemitism
and Hitler are taken for granted throughout the story. As Aaron
Greidinger, the young writer who tells the story, says: " 'The Jews
in Poland are trapped. . . . I know for sure that we will all be
destroyed' " (131). Morris Feitelzohn, Aaron's friend, warns him to

113

get out of Poland however he can because " 'A holocaust is coming
here that will be worse than in Chmielnitsky's time' " (151).

Hopeless and helpless before this terrible fate, nearly all of the
Jews in the novel live only for the present, pursuing pleasure without regard for truth or value. "We all," confesses Aaron, "lived for
the present—the whole Jewish community" (241). The novel
abounds with hedonistic schemes, epitomized by Morris Feitelzohn's ambition to establish a school of hedonism. Aaron says of the
American Yiddish actress Betty Slonim, one of his numerous wom-
en, that " 'She wants the same thing we all do—to grab some pleasure before we vanish forever' " (59). Aaron understands only too
clearly that the search for happiness is an insatiable appetite which
grows by what it feeds on, and that for anyone but a pig the question
" 'Am I happy?' " must always be answered in the negative. *Fastidio
ergo sum* must be the motto of the discriminating sybarite. "I stood
and asked myself, 'Are you happy now?' I waited for an answer from
that deep source called the inner being, the ego, the superego, the
spirit . . . but no answer came" (63). The most intrepid pursuers
of pleasure are the characters who speak obsessively of suicide. This
is especially the case with Aaron himself and with Betty (who
eventually does take her own life). Suicides are cast by Singer as
hedonists who have overreached themselves and aspired to more
(and more intense) pleasures than they are capable of achieving.

The self-destructive futility of hedonism is hardly a new theme
in Singer's novels. But whereas in the earlier novels the distance
established by moral judgment between the novelist and the hedonists was clear and distinct, here it is blurred by what we may
suppose to be the unwillingness of the novelist to separate himself
completely from his own youthful experiences and aspirations. In
his old age, Singer appears to have succumbed to a kind of vanity
which boasts of the very exploits which his better self has throughout
his career treated contemptuously. In *Shosha*, as in *A Young Man
in Search of Love*, the subject of sex is a virtual obsession. "In all
the novels I had read, the heroes desired only one woman, but here
I was, lusting after the whole female gender" (87). Aaron tells us
how he simultaneously carried on affairs with the Communist Dora
Stolnitz, with Celia Chentshiner, a married woman, with Betty
Slonim, the mistress of the American millionaire Sam Dreiman, and
with the Polish maid Tekla. We can well imagine that poor Aaron,
just like the Singer of the autobiographical memoir, was so "sated

with sex" that he occasionally longed for a night of restful sleep
alone in his bed.

In that same memoir Singer recalls how he "frequently fantasized
about writing a novel in which the hero was simultaneously in love
with a number of women" (36). He has now realized that fantasy
several times, most notably in *Enemies*. But whereas in *The Magician of Lublin* and *Enemies* each of the hero's women represented
some distinct portion of his fragmented life, in *Shosha* the multi-
plication of lovers seems more a virtuoso performance than a struc-
tural and thematic device. The following passage is, alas, typical:
"During one night I had found my lost love and then succumbed
to temptation and betrayed her. I had stolen the concubine of my
benefactor, lied to her, aroused her passion by telling her all my
lusty adventures, and made her confess sins that filled me with
disgust. I had been impotent and then turned into a sexual giant"
(86). The more Aaron—a wayward yeshiva student—recounts his
sexual exploits, the more the reader is likely to share the doubts
of Bellow's Artur Sammler regarding the fitness of Jews for "this
erotic Roman voodoo primitivism. He questioned whether release
from long Jewish mental discipline, hereditary training in lawful
control, was obtainable upon individual application." (76)

Ultimately, despite the unseemly relish with which he dwells on
what must finally be repudiated, this is also the view of the narrator
and his creator as well. It is clear not only that sexuality stands in
diametrical opposition to Judaism, but that it derives much of its
demonic force from the power of what might be called anti-Judaism.
When Aaron takes Betty to visit the Krochmalna ghetto in which
he had grown up, they enter an empty prayer house and approach
the holy ark: "I pulled apart the curtain before the ark, opened the
door, and glanced at the scrolls in their velvet mantelets and the
gold embroidery tarnished with the years. Betty and I thrust our
heads inside. Her face was hot. We shared a sinful urge to desecrate
the sacred and we kissed" (72). Even a mode of activity which at
its inception is intended to overcome the despair that accompanies
loss of faith turns into a perverse acknowledgment of the power of
the lapsed faith.

In the book, it is primarily (though, as we shall see, not exclusively) religion which resists hedonism. Religion reacts to the imminence of the Holocaust not by living in and for the present, but
by dwelling on the past. "In Germany, Hitler had solidified his

power, but the Warsaw Jews had celebrated the festival of the exodus out of Egypt four thousand years ago" (69). The very fact that they live thus in the past implies their belief in a future. Hitlers and Stalins, like Pharaohs and Chmielnickis, come and wreak havoc and then disappear, are blotted out; but the Jewish people is eternal.

Yet Aaron, like Singer the son of a Chasidic rabbi and beneficiary of a religious education, has wandered far from Judaism and its world view. When he was growing up, Judaism struck him as mostly deprivations and prohibitions. There were no toys, only the father's books, in which he was constantly engrossed; and the books seemed to yield infinite variations of "Thou shalt not." "From the time I can first remember, I heard him repeat the phrase 'It is forbidden.' Everything I wanted to do was a transgression. I was not allowed to draw or paint a person—that violated the Second Commandment. I couldn't say a word against another boy—that was slander. I couldn't laugh at anyone—that was mockery. I couldn't make up a story—that represented a lie" (5). When, during the first World War, Warsaw was simultaneously invaded by the Germans and by Enlightenment, young Aaron was taken captive by the latter. Of course he took his new captivity to be freedom, from the yoke of Jewish laws and restrictions. But eventually he learns the paradox whereby, as Feitelzohn says, " 'This alleged freedom has transformed me into a slave' " (20).

If there are any benefits to be reaped from his emancipation from religion, Aaron has not discovered them. "From the day I had left my father's house I had existed in a state of perpetual despair. Occasionally, I considered the notion of repentance, of returning to real Jewishness. But to live like my father, my grandfathers, and great-grandfathers, without their faith—was this possible?" (183). Although Aaron the writer and roué has long since left his father's house and religion, his father—though dead—has not left him. When he is on the verge of accepting the ailing Sam Dreiman's proposal that he, Aaron—in return for a visa to America—marry Sam's mistress Betty so that they may all comfort· one another in a *ménage à trois,* a voice cries within him: " 'Run! . . . You'll sink into a slime from which you'll never be able to get out. They'll drag you into the abyss!' It was my father's voice" (158).

If Judaism is a form of faith which Aaron Greidinger admires but cannot share, Communism is a substitute religion which he neither shares nor wishes to share. In *A Young Man in Search of Love,*

Singer recalls how, in the 1920s, he was "surrounded on all sides
by the faithful who all believed in something. . ." (40). But this is
not quite the picture of Polish Jewry which *Shosha* gives us, for
here the predominant impression these characters give is one of
hedonism, lassitude, nihilism. But primary among the faithful from
whom Aaron is estranged by his sceptical pessimism are the Communists. These true believers are epitomized by his lover Dora
Stolnitz, whose great goal in life is to settle in Soviet Russia, the
socialist utopia. Dora's "big, fluttering eyes" are her only attractive
physical feature, reflecting as they do "a blend of cunning and the
solemnity of one who has assumed the mission of saving mankind"
(37).

It is, of course, axiomatic in Singer (in addition to being true) that
the pseudoreligious desire to help "mankind" invariably leads to
cruelty on a massive scale. This is because the worship of mankind
is nothing other than idolatry, and idolatry is always cruel and
pitiless. "Every idol," writes Cynthia Ozick, "is a shadow of Moloch,
demanding human flesh to feed on. The deeper the devotion to the
idol, the more pitiless in tossing it its meal will be the devotee."[2]
Dora is partly disillusioned about the land in which she had supposed life to be starting anew when she learns that her best friend
has been shot by the Soviets and that whole groups of her comrades
who had gone to that promised land had been imprisoned, tortured,
exiled to Siberia. After surviving an attempt at suicide, she decides
to share her disillusionment and misery with another survivor of
the Russian "experiment," a writer named Felhendler. Aaron had
known him as the most ruthless of Communist idolators, who would
warn fellow writers that they would be hanged from the nearest
lamp post once the revolution came. His hegira to the USSR had
ended in imprisonment and torture.

When, after a long separation, Aaron meets the chastened Dora
and Felhendler, he finds that although they have been disillusioned
with Stalin and their Communist ardor burns with a very subdued
flame, they have not penetrated to the quick of this ulcer. They still
"believe" in revolution, but now their hopes are attached to Trotsky
instead of Stalin. They have yet to grasp the first principles of the
idolatry they serve: namely, that revolutions are synonymous with
bloodshed and that a fanatical devotion to "mankind" leads inevitably to terror. They have also yet to recognize, as even the pro-
fessedly irreligious Aaron does, the sinfulness of human nature,

even in its "proletarian" form. " 'Dora, you speak of the masses as if they were innocent lambs and only a few villains are responsible for the human tragedy. Actually, a large part of the masses themselves want to kill, plunder, rape. . . . Chmielnitsky's Cossacks weren't capitalists, neither were Petlura's murderers' " (206).

Aaron has experienced both the mindlessness and ruthlessness of the Communists in his professional capacity, as a Yiddish writer. Both before and after her disillusionment with Stalin, Dora condemns all literature which does not concentrate on the plight of the poor as a flight into "unreality" and worse. Reminding Aaron to take his "Fascist manuscripts" out of her apartment before she departs for Russia, Dora exhorts him: " 'It's never too late to accept the truth. Spit on all this slime and come with me. Stop writing about those rabbis and spirits and see what the real world looks like. Everything here is corrupt. Over there life is beginning' " (40).

Questions about the nature and function of literature are central to *Shosha*. It is easy enough for Aaron to see that the Communist definitions are false, harder to discover which are true. His original commitment to literature was based on his conviction that its aim was "to prevent time from vanishing." Yet he is resistant to writing about his own time because he wishes to startle the world but lives in an age already jaded with monstrosities more fantastic than any imagination could have invented: ". . . What could startle the world? No crime, no misery, no sexual perversion, no madness. Twenty million people had perished in the Great War, and here the world was preparing for another conflagration" (25). Aaron also fears that he is writing in a language that is itself in danger of vanishing. The Yiddish writer felt isolated and frustrated not only because his choice of such a vocation made him a *meshumad* (apostate) in the eyes of the religious, but also because he was "stuck with a language and culture no one recognized outside of a small circle of Yiddishists and radicals" (16). This was a sort of double exile. Religious Jews were not conciliated by the fact that you used Hebrew letters to write about secular, "European" subjects; but those same Hebrew letters decisively shut you out from the world of secular European culture.

Aaron's primary literary endeavor in the first half of the novel is a play entitle *The Maiden from Ludmir*. Although Aaron knows that the Yiddish theater is the best means of reaching the audience that exists beyond the confines of Yiddishism and radicalism, he does not at first intend the play to be performed. But his meeting with Betty Slonim, the Russian-born American actress who has come to Poland with her elderly millionaire keeper Sam Dreiman in order to star in the Yiddish theater, changes Aaron's mind. The subject of Aaron's play is a girl who (like many of Singer's female characters) wanted to live like a man, and therefore studied the Torah, wore ritual fringes and prayer shawl, donned phylacteries, and preached to Chasidim.[3] The reason alleged for her peculiarities is that she was possessed by two dybbuks, one of a whore, the other of a musician. Hearing this description, Betty sees the role as a good "vehicle" for the display of her talents—provided, of course, that it be written (and rewritten) according to her specifications.

The Yiddish theater requires the young writer to sully his art with commercial and personal considerations. Feitelzohn tells Aaron that his fortune (in love as well as money) is made if he will only pack his play " 'with all the love and sex it can take.' " When Aaron expresses his reluctance to turn the play into trash, Feitelzohn chides him: " 'Theater is trash by definition. There's no such thing as a sustaining literary play. . . . The main thing is, don't spare the schmaltz. Today's Jews like three things—sex, Torah, and revolution, all mixed together. Give them those and they'll raise you to the skies' " (33). Singer's picture of the Yiddish theater is not wholly unattractive, for the *shund* (trash) exists alongside a considerable vitality and folk intimacy. But Aaron, despite the advances he receives (in money from Sam and in another form from Betty), cannot make his peace with the high-flown vulgarity of the Yiddish stage, and production of the play is cancelled.

It turns out later that even Aaron has not been wholly unmindful of the attacks on his play (not all of which emanate from Communists) for not reflecting the tragic situation of Polish Jewry and the imminent danger of Hitlerism. But (and this is obviously true of Singer's own career) Aaron chooses not to approach these subjects directly and wishes to gain the perspective on the present which is available only by studying the past. He begins a novel about Jacob Frank, the false messiah, and then is offered the chance to write a serialized biography of Frank in a newspaper. This time Aaron's literary efforts do succeed in reaching a large audience, much to the consternation of the leftists, who "still complained that this kind of writing was an opiate for the masses" (230). But in fact all writing about false messiahs is for Aaron (as for Singer himself) writing about

Hitler and Stalin as well. His second novel (like Singer's first) deals
with the earlier false messiah Sabbatai Zevi, and describes "with
much detail the Jewish longing for redemption in an epoch that
displayed similarities to our own. What Hitler threatened to do to
the Jews Bogdan Chmielnitsky had done some three hundred years
earlier" (233). Thus does his rabbinical father's view of history receive confirmation in the novel by the wayward son. That is why
even ignorant and unworldly Shosha can exclaim, upon reading her
beloved's fiction about the Jews of the seventeenth century: " 'Oh,
Mommy, it's exactly like today!' " (232).

Even at its best, however, the literary vocation cannot provide
a substitute for the life-giving bread of the Jewish religion, of which
Aaron has deprived himself. Even if writers were not—as they are—
a treacherous group, even if the Yiddish theatre were not—as it
is—trash, literature can never take the place of religion. When he
reflects on his dismal life among emancipated belles-lettrists and
enlighteners, Aaron castigates himself for having " 'thrown away
four thousand years of Jewishness and exchanged it for meaningless
literature, Yiddishism, Feitelzohnism.' " Neither his pursuit of pleasure nor his flight from religion can succeed, the former because
it grows by what it feeds on, the latter because " 'We are running
away and Mount Sinai runs after us' " (255–56).

Unable either to escape God or to return to Him, immersed in
hedonism yet revolted by it, committed to a literary career yet
aware of its inability to supply the spiritual nourishment he craves,
Aaron Greidinger—to the astonishment and consternation of all his
friends—executes a great leap backward by marrying his childhood
sweetheart, Shosha Schuldiener. While on a sightseeing tour of his
old neighborhood with Betty, Aaron meets Shosha and is astonished
to find that she has neither grown nor aged nor even altered her
wardrobe in the twenty years since their last meeting. When asked
what he can possibly see in this physically and mentally backward
girl, arrested at the stage of childhood, Aaron answers: " 'I see
myself' " (81). Not, to be sure, himself as he has become but himself
as he would have been if time had stood still and he had remained
within the confines, mental as well as physical, of the ghetto. Unlike
his other lovers, especially Celia, who dwell on death, Shosha seems
to have found a magical way to stop the advance of time and so deny
death. For Aaron to marry her is a double denial of death because
it means that he is forfeiting the chance to save his life with the

visa that Betty offers. He refers to Shosha as his child, but also as
the "chaste Jewish daughter" he knows his own mother to have
been when she was a girl.

This is but one of many instances in the novel which treat of the
intimate relation between the present and the past. We have already
noticed that Aaron's dead father speaks to him at a crucial moment
in his life, and that characters are constantly being struck by the
parallels between their own era and that of the Jews of the seventeenth century. The recrudescence of death in life, and the ambiguous relation between the living and the dead, obsess many of
the characters in *Shosha*. Betty says to Aaron that " 'the past generations are our dybbuks. . . . A person is literally a cemetery where
multitudes of living corpses are buried' " (205). This means not only
that there is a kind of life after death, but that there is also death
in the midst of life, and that the fullness of our being depends upon
the integration of our present, conscious life with the layers of being
which we inherit from those who have preceded us. " 'How,' " asks
Haiml, " 'can it be that all the generations are dead and only we
shlemiels are allegedly living?' " (269).

What saves all this speculation from being, like some other speculation in the book, idle is the omnipresence of death in the Holocaust which will engulf most of the characters, and in the
resurrection, in body and soul in a few cases, in memory in most,
of these Polish Jews in the Land of Israel. Once, while musing upon
the frivolous, wasted lives of himself and his friends, Aaron spec-
ulates that "the generations that will come after us . . . will think
that we all went to our death in repentance. They will consider all
of us holy martyrs. . . . Actually, every one of us will die with the
same passions he lived with" (256). This appears at first to be an
acerbic comment on the tendency to sentimentalize the Jewish life
of Eastern Europe because it was so brutally destroyed by the
Germans, as well as on the post-Holocaust tradition which declares
that all the Jewish victims of Hitler died for *kiddush hashem* (sanc-
tification of the [divine] name) and are therefore to be revered as
martyrs. Yet, in the book's epilogue, which is set in Israel thirteen
years later, we are permitted no ironical superiority to the characters
who report that the imminence of death did have a transforming
effect upon many of Aaron's gloomy, cynical, and immoral friends.
Celia, we learn, " 'wasn't the same Celia any more. Our situation
. . . uplifted her to a degree that can't be put into words. She

became beautiful!' " (270). Even in Morris Feitelzohn the immediacy of a Jewish martyr's death had awakened the dead souls of his
ancestors and raised him above the secular triviality of his worldly
existence. " 'He talked those nights as I never heard him talk before.
The heritage of generations had wakened within him, and he hurled
sulphur and brimstone against the Almighty; at the same time the
words themselves blazed with a religious fire' " (271).

Israel is the most appropriate place in which to speculate on the
possibility of resurrection of the dead. If the most terrible collective
death of the Jewish People in their long history can be followed by
the rebirth, after nearly two thousand years, of an independent
Jewish state in the Land of Israel, who can rule out the possibility
that " 'the dead *will* be resurrected' " (269)? Haiml is at least certain
that the souls of the dead Jews he knew—Celia, Morris, Shosha—
have come to rest in Israel, the one place left in the world where
they can truly be mourned, remembered, and perhaps raised up
again. He lives with them more than with his living neighbors.

Aaron records these Zionist views sympathetically, but withholds
his assent. His rescue, effected by an American Army colonel whom
Betty married after she left Poland, took him to New York via
Shanghai. He only visits Israel, as a writer who has achieved fame
in the "good" Diaspora, the United States. His primary commitment
is still to literature. When, thirteen years earlier, he had paid what
turned out to be his last visit to the Jewish section of Warsaw, he
had sensed that the end of that world was near, and "I tried to
engrave in my memory each alley, each building, each store, each
face. I thought that this was how a condemned man would be looking
at the world on his way to the gallows" (257). In Aaron as in Singer
himself the attempt to resurrect Jewish life in Israel, one of the
most extraordinary instances of national rebirth in history, does not
strike a fully responsive chord. Rather, he chooses to make of literature itself the instrument for preserving the memory, and res-
urrecting the souls, of the dead. But neither for him nor for his old
friends now living in Israel does there exist a sufficient and convincing answer to the question of why a whole world had to be
destroyed and so much unspeakable suffering endured; and the
novel ends in darkness and in doubt:

"There can't be any answer for suffering—not for the sufferer."
"In that case, what am I waiting for?"

Genia opened the door. "Why are you two sitting in the dark, eh?"
Haiml laughed. "We're waiting for an answer." (277)

CHAPTER 9

The Short Stories

They hated him for the amazing thing that had happened to him—his fame—but this they never referred to. Instead they discussed his style: his Yiddish was impure, his sentences lacked grace and sweep, his paragraph transitions were amateur, vile. Or else they raged against his subject-matter, which was insanely sexual, pornographic, paranoid, freakish—men who embraced men, women who caressed women, sodomists of every variety, boys copulating with hens, butchers who drank blood for strength behind the knife. All the stories were set in an imaginary Polish village, Zwrdl, and by now there was almost no American literary intellectual alive who had not learned to say Zwrdl when he meant "lewd."

—Cynthia Ozick, "Envy; or, Yiddish in America"

IRVING Howe has often remarked upon the paradox whereby the very modernism which arouses suspicion and resentment among Yiddish readers of Singer's fiction has been the basis of his extraordinary and (for a Yiddish writer) unparalleled popularity among literary intellectuals whose ignorance of Yiddish is equalled by their indifference to such parochial Jewish concerns as national survival. Howe points out that many intelligent and experienced Yiddish writers are uneasy, even impatient and angry, with Singer's work because of his "heavy stress upon sexuality . . . concern for the irrational, expressionist distortions of character," and his total indifference to the Yiddishist traditions of sentimentality and social justice. Among devotees of literary modernism, however, "for whom the determination not to be shocked has become a point of honor,"[1] these same characteristics have contributed as much to his high reputation as the less accidental traits of stylistic brilliance and narrative invention.

The modernism which has brought such differing reactions from the Yiddish and the non-Yiddish reading audiences is contained

124

mainly in Singer's voluminous output of short stories. The novels operate within the old-fashioned traditions of nineteenth-century realism and deal, unmistakably, with questions of the national destiny of the Jewish people. Although it may not be correct to read the short stories as modernist excursions into diabolism, perversity, and apocalypse, entirely cut off from Singer's novelistic concerns with Jewish religion and Jewish destiny, we can hardly doubt that this is how they are generally read. Whatever may be the reasons for Singer's popularity as a short-story writer with the readers of the *New Yorker, Playboy,* and *Esquire,* it is safe to assume that a passionate interest in things Jewish and in the tragic course of Jewish history is not among them. The hordes of students who flock to hear Singer at places like Charlottesville, Virginia, or Madison, Wisconsin, may reasonably be supposed to have a keener interest in dybbuks and spooks than in the destroyed Jewish world of Eastern Europe. There may even be a dark political significance in the fact that some of the most ecstatic praise of Singer's modernist brilliance as a short-story writer has appeared in such journals as the *New York Review of Books,* which nobody ever accused of an undue concern with the well-being of Jews.

Nevertheless, the wide appeal of Singer's stories among readers ignorant of, and indifferent to, Jewish religion, Jewish history, Jewish peoplehood, is a literary fact of the first importance because it disproves the fashionable literary prejudice which holds that writing about Jews is an insuperable obstacle to universal appeal. Critics who have blithely assumed that it is the natural destiny of the human race, or of that part of it which reads books, to puzzle over Blake's Zoas and Yeats's gyres and Pound's socioeconomic ravings, are invariably brought up short at the prospect of reading books about Jews because, they maintain, the concerns of Jews are not those of universal humanity. Anyone familiar with the body of criticism about the writings of Saul Bellow (not excluding some of that writer's unhappy utterances about his own work) will know that it is one of the smelly little orthodoxies of American literary criticism that the Jewish writer (and he alone) is compelled to choose between writing about the experience of his people and addressing himself to the principle of Mankind and therefore to humanity as a whole.

Singer writes almost always as a Jew, to Jews, for Jews; and yet he is heard by everybody. The audience of Yiddishists often resents him for some of the reasons that it resented Sholem Asch: getting

translated, succeeding in reaching the great public through translation, and then writing *for* translation. But not even this resentful
and suspicious body of readers can accuse him of doing as Asch
seemed to them to do, writing explicitly Christian stories in order
to gain a wide audience. Singer's tremendous success among critics
as well as ordinary readers seems to illustrate the truth of Cynthia
Ozick's contention that, contrary to the apostles (to the Jews, any-
way) of universalism, great literature never consciously seeks to be
"universal": "Dante made literature out of an urban vernacular,
Shakespeare spoke to a small island people, Tolstoy brooded on
upper-class Russians, Yeats was the kindling for a Dublin-confined
renascence. They did not intend to address the principle of Mankind; each was, if you will allow the infamous word, tribal. Literature
does not spring from the urge to Esperanto, but from the tribe."[2]
Singer himself has always recognized that it was only by examining,
and not by avoiding, his own memories and experiences as a Jew
that he could penetrate to the memories and experiences of mankind, which is an infinitely varied repetition. He once stated in an
interview that "we Jews have been living in an eternal, permanent
crisis. Life itself is a permanent crisis, but the Jews really live in
a more permanent crisis."[3]

    In order to give some idea of the range and variety of Singer's
short stories I have selected for discussion some representative tales
in four of his favorite modes: the apocalyptic mode; the celebration
of Jewish survival; the story of love, excess, and perversion; and the
autobiographical tale. This is a sampling, not a scheme of classifi-
cation. If it were the latter, we would have to devote a separate
discussion to Singer's tales of the supernatural and the grotesque,
which have often been dealt with by critics as a distinctive element
of his work. But if we think, as Singer has urged us to do, of his
demons and his Satan as representing "the ways of the world,"[4]
their uniqueness as a subject (if not as a mode of grotesque narration)
is considerably lessened. Finally, I have treated "Gimpel the Fool,"
Singer's greatest story, as *sui generis*, a class unto itself.

I   *Apocalyptic Tales*

    "The Gentleman from Cracow" (in *Gimpel the Fool and Other
Stories*) contains within itself several of the most typical elements
of Singer's short fiction. On the surface, it is an unironic morality

tale unimpeachably based on a "parchment chronicle" signed by "trustworthy witnesses." The town of Frampol, beset by poverty and drought, is tempted into gross transgressions of the Law to obtain the gold which the wealthy newcomer, allegedly a doctor from Cracow, has brought. When he suggests so un-Jewish an activity as a ball, Rabbi Ozer warns his flock that they are being led astray by the Evil One. But the wisdom of Torah can no longer penetrate the skulls of young men thinking only of the ball and of the women to be seen there. At the ball, the Croesus from Cracow offers to enrich the whole community on condition that, by lottery, every girl provide herself with a husband before midnight. He himself, in accordance with the Cinderella pattern of the story, draws a lascivious harlot named Hodle. She, like a number of similar women in Singer's fictional world, has sinned throughout her life, and not for bread, but " 'for the sheer pleasure.' " The specifically anti-Jewish character of sexual promiscuity and excess is emphasized by the groom's blasphemous parody of the formula recited to the bride during a Jewish marriage ceremony: " 'With this ring, be thou desecrated to me according to the blasphemy of Korah and Ishmael' "(38–39).

Only one person present at this festival of abominations sees what it portends. He is an old man who warns the Jews of the wrath to come: " 'A fire is upon us, burning, Jews, Satan's fire. Save your souls, Jews. Flee, before it is too late!' "(38). But he is treated like most bearers of ill tidings to the Jews: he is gagged and expelled— and proven correct.[5] Hardly has he left the scene when a bolt of lightning strikes the study house, the ritual bath, and the synagogue simultaneously, setting the whole town on fire. Having witnessed all this, even the townspeople of Frampol can hardly be surprised when the gentleman from Cracow reveals himself to be the Chief of the Devils, Ketev Mriri, and his bride turns out to be Lilith.

All of Frampol, except for the rabbi's house, is consumed by fire, and most of the inhabitants find themselves naked and floundering in mud, fitting symbol of the sexual excess in which they have been mired. Yet the rabbi's passionate exhortations to resist evil and his courageous offer of himself as a scapegoat for the community's sins do have their effect, and only one among the great multitude of sinners loses his life. Nevertheless, great loss of life there is, for as so often happens it is the innocent and not the guilty who suffer. In a passage which echoes *The Family Moskat's* reproach of Jews who lead their own children to the slaughterhouse, the narrator reveals that "it was the infants who had been the real victims of the passion for gold that had caused the inhabitants of Frampol to transgress. The infants' cribs were burned, their little bones were charred"(43). This is an especially painful punishment for the people of Frampol because, throughout their years of wretched poverty and endless bad fortune, they had always "been blessed with fine children"(24).

But the catastrophe brings in its wake more than punishment and makes of "The Gentleman from Cracow" something other than a moral tale. The fire proves to be an apocalyptic event, the massacre of the innocent children a prelude to Frampol's entry into a better way of life, even a new world. The paradoxical outcome of so much greed, lust, and blasphemy is compassion, charity, diligence, cooperation, and reconstruction: all of which had been little in evidence before the arrival of the gentleman–devil from Cracow. The lust for gold is permanently stifled: "From generation to generation the people remained paupers. A gold coin became an abomination in Frampol, and even silver was looked at askance"(44). This is one of Singer's apocalyptic tales in which the dangerous theory that "worse is better" is endorsed by the action. Yet the paradox has been invoked—perhaps this is the ultimate irony—in order to confirm the traditional theology which holds that out of evil must come good, and that even the most enterprising of devils is a servant of heaven.

"The Destruction of Kreshev" (in *The Spinoza of Market Street*) may be viewed as pendent or counterpoint to "The Gentleman from Cracow" among Singer's tales in the apocalyptic mode. For this story, narrated by Satan himself, is an oblique but harsh criticism of the apocalyptic temper, and particularly the belief that "worse is better," that the path to virtue is paved with excess, and that catastrophe is the necessary antecedent to Messianic redemption. Here too (as in so many Singer stories of every mode and voice) it is sex which both precipitates and contains within itself all other sins; and here too it is the innocent children of the town who are the primary victims of the lust of their elders. But "The Destruction of Kreshev," like *Satan in Goray*, does not encourage us to rest in the comforting paradox that out of evil comes good, out of defilement, purity, out of wickedness, redemption.

Whereas the gentleman from Cracow involves a whole community in sin, the chief sinners here are distinct individuals whose careers are traced for us in some detail before they take their plunge into perversion and defilement. Lise, the central figure of the tale, bears some resemblance to the heroine of "Yentl the Yeshiva Boy," for she can hardly bake a potato but is as adept as the cleverest man in the study of Scripture and Talmud. Her other peculiarity is an excess of modesty. When her father Reb Bunim— a wealthy, virtuous, and sweet-tempered man—asks her (at age fifteen) to choose between two prospective husbands, a tall, handsome, rich man from Lublin who is a mediocre scholar, and an undersized and homely Talmudic prodigy from Warsaw, her intellectualism and her prudishness direct her to the latter. This miracle of erudition, whose name is Shloimele, dazzles the Kreshev Jews with his intellectual pyrotechnics. Readers of Yiddish literature will recognize him as a blood brother to Peretz's Chananiah, who in the great story "Devotion without End" epitomizes the false scholars who come to the Torah "not for its own sake or from love of God but out of a lust to shine in their own right." Singer chooses to associate this peculiarly Jewish lust with another, more generally available kind.

Once they are married, the clever Shloimele lures his loving wife into the study of Kabbalah, into sexual research and experimentation, into animalism. It is specifically his intellectualism which is responsible for an impotence which can only be assuaged by imaginings of infidelity and perversion. The dedication to evil of this Talmudic scholar is, however, of the most high-minded sort, for he is a disciple of the long-dead false Messiah Sabbatai Zevi, and shares his master's belief that an excess of degradation means greater sanctity, and the more heinous the wickedness the closer the day of redemption. " 'Since this generation cannot become completely pure, let it grow completely impure!' " (191). His own plunge into the abyss is justified as the necessary prelude to sublimity, his energetic devotion to sin as the means of burning through all those passions which must be consummated before the Messiah can come. Just as his master Sabbatai Zevi had converted to Islam in order (so his dutiful followers believed) to go into that pit of defilement from which the divine sparks had to be rescued, so does Shloimele threaten to convert to Roman Catholicism.

The instrument for Shloimele's realization of his perverse ambitions is the coachman Mendel. Mendel, like many Jews before and since, has chosen to become Esau and to forsake his own heritage. He completely disregards Jewish laws and customs, dedicates himself to lechery, and espouses a wholly materialistic view of life which pays no heed to threats of what may await him in the world to come. Shloimele forces Lise into adultery with Mendel after persuading her that she and the coachman are reincarnations of, respectively, Abishag the Shunammite, and Adonijah, the son of Haggith. Lise's ruination, we are again reminded by the Satanic narrator, is caused by her husband's overdeveloped intellect. "In truth, Shloimele, the villain, devised this whim merely to satisfy his own depraved passions, since he had grown perverse from too much thinking . . ."(197). Unlike the stories in which what Morris Golden calls the "Spinoza" theme[6] is dominant and the flatulent, dyspeptic thinker (e.g. Dr. Fischelson) must be cured of his cerebral illness by sexual union with an unintellectual female, "The Destruction of Kreshev" makes intellectual imbalance the immediate cause of sexual depravity.

At the point of his most intense eagerness to break out of the old world into the new, regardless of the price to be paid in mere "temporal" affliction, Shloimele had said: " 'I love fire! I love a holocaust . . . I would like the whole world to burn . . . ' "(192). When the abominations of Shloimele, Lise, and Mendel are made public, the town's rabbi declares that he is in truth not the rabbi of Kreshev but of Sodom and Gomorrah, the Biblical cities which were destroyed by fire from above because all their inhabitants had become wicked. But the analogy is inexact. Kreshev's abominations have been committed only by three people, but even after Mendel is punished and Lise hangs herself, the town and its inhabitants are destroyed by fire and plague. The holocaust beloved of apocalyptic desperadoes does indeed materialize, but the promised redemption is nowhere in evidence at the end of the tale. If, in "The Gentleman from Cracow," Singer has paid grudging respect to the good which may sometimes result from demonic energy, here he reasserts his more characteristic suspicion of false Messianism in its multifarious forms.

II *Tales of Survival*

In 1933 Singer published the first of what might be called miracle tales which celebrate Jewish survival and, by taking for granted the timelessness of biblical archetypes, declare that Jews, throughout their long history, have never really changed. "The Old Man" (in *Gimpel the Fool and Other Stories*) tells the tale of the nonagenarian Reb Moshe Ber, who has managed, but only barely, to survive both his children and his grandchildren. He had come to Warsaw from Jozefow just before the outbreak of the Great War to live with his prosperous son. But two years later the war ravaged the family, leaving only the old man, who must now retrace his steps and return to his Turisk Chasidim in Jozefow.

Enduring intense cold and almost unrelieved hunger, even convinced at times that he is already dead, the ancient Moshe Ber makes his way by foot across war-torn Europe, through Galicia, Zamosc, Bilgoray, and finally back to the home he had left. Nothing in the narrative of his suffering and deprivation and ultimate rescue departs from surface realism, even naturalism: yet the story culminates in a miracle, which is taken entirely for granted by the old man. The Turisk Chasidim, almost at a loss to know how to express their gratitude for his safe return to them, arrange Moshe Ber's marriage to a forty-year-old deaf and dumb village girl. "Exactly nine months later she gave birth to a son—now he had someone to say *kaddish* for him." With perfect self-possession, Moshe Ber names the child Isaac, reveals that he is now a hundred years old, and reminds his friends that the miracle of Jewish survival is as real and living as ever it was. " 'And Abraham was a hundred years old,' he recited, 'when his son Isaac was born unto him. And Sarah said: "God hath made me laugh so that all who hear will laugh with me" ' "(159). The meaning of the whole story bursts forth in its stunning conclusion. Those present at the miracle laugh not merely because of the age of Moshe Ber-Abraham, but at the sheer madness of the Jewish faith that, despite all catastrophe, despite the destruction of millions of individuals, the Jewish *people* will live.

"The Little Shoemakers" (in *Gimpel the Fool . . .*) is one of Singer's most beautiful stories and also one of his most ambitious. At once a mourning over what has been lost and a celebration of what has survived, it tries to encompass within a few pages the enormous upheavals which have gripped the Jews in modern times. Irving Howe says that this story "sums up the whole of contemporary Jewish experience: from tradition to modernity, from the old country to the new, from the ghetto to the camps."[7] Perhaps because it is dealing with events that defy credibility and have almost always proved resistant to naturalistic representation, the story comes much closer to the formal devices of archetype and allegory than do most of Singer's tales. It thus collapses the most cataclysmic historical events—pogroms, mass migrations of unprecedented magnitude, the Holocaust—into the fable of three generations of a single family transplanted from a shtetl of Eastern Europe to the New World.

Like many of Singer's tales, "The Little Shoemakers" commences in the aftermath of Chmielnitzki's pogroms in the seventeenth century. But it moves quickly to modern times and to Abba, like his ancestors a righteous shoemaker (whose surname—Shuster—names his occupation). Abba lives his life in Frampol within the traditional bounds of Jewish faith. His learning is wholly religious and completely unmediated by a sense of historical distance. He can identify with Noah, still more with Abraham. Indeed, "he often thought that if the Almighty were to call on him to sacrifice his eldest son, Gimpel, he would rise early in the morning and carry out his commands without delay." Abba believes that he, like all the Jews since the destruction of the Second Temple, lives in exile, far from the homeland in Eretz Israel, because he has sinned, and not because God has been unfaithful or powerless. But he is sustained in exile by his knowledge of the unbroken continuity between himself and the Patriarchs—"as if he too were part of the Bible"(92–93). This apparently fantastic belief is thoroughly confirmed by the biblical magnitude of the events through which Abba, like all the Jews of Europe, is destined to live. These are indeed biblical times.

But although he awaits the Redemption, and will be ready to leave for the Holy Land when the Messiah comes, Abba's attachments to the place where he lives in exile are as intricate and traditional as we might expect them to be in a people who, like the Jews, had lived in Poland for eight hundred years. Though his house is in bad repair, he resists his wife Pesha's recommendation to tear it down and build a new one. He would rather keep things as they are, because he "found it hard to part with the home in which his parents and grandparents, and the whole family, stretching back for generations, had lived and died." Abba understands that the fullness of life is an accumulation of memories, preserved to us by material objects, apparently dead yet resonant with the life of the past. "The walls were like an album in which the fortunes of the family had been recorded." The Book of Memory is almost as sacred to Abba as the Five Books of Moses. No, he decides, "there was nothing to change. Let everything stand as it had stood for ages"(98–99).

But Abba is unable to transmit either his wisdom or his contentment to his sons. No sooner has he made his commitment to standing still than his son Gimpel announces his intention to go to America. He wants enlightenment and American plumbing, both of which are in short supply in Frampol. Although Gimpel's parting is bitter, the tone of his letters from America is conciliatory—and satisfied as well. He proudly reports that there, unlike Poland, "No one walks with his eyes on the ground, everybody holds his head high"(103). Gimpel induces his brother Getzel to follow him, Getzel brings over Treitel, and so on until all seven brothers have left, seven Jews of the approximately two million who, during four decades starting in the 1880s, came from Eastern Europe to the United States. But Abba and his wife Pesha, though bereft of their sons, can see no reason to move from one corner of the Diaspora to another, more alien one.

For forty years, during which time he loses Pesha, Abba resists the pleadings of his sons to join them in America, and consoles himself with work at the shoemaker's bench. But the next upheaval in the life of Eastern European Jewry sweeps even Abba away from his traditional moorings. As Hitler's barbarians descend upon Poland, Abba assumes that the deliverance from exile, so long delayed, is finally at hand. "One morning, while Abba was wandering among his thoughts, he heard a tremendous crash. The old man shook in his bones: the blast of the Messiah's trumpet. He dropped the boot he had been working on and ran out in ecstasy. But it was not Elijah the Prophet proclaiming the Messiah. Nazi planes were bombing Frampol"(108). Abba is indeed, like the Patriarchs, living in biblical times, but the only Messiah,as Hertz Yanovar insists at the end of *The Family Moskat,* is death. Abba, who from his youth had been ready, like Abraham, to heed the command to get out of his country, now does indeed abandon the house of his forefathers and the place of his birth, just as Abraham had done; only he does so, not at the behest of God, but to save his life.

The fifth part of "The Little Shoemakers" stresses more insistently than any other the degree to which the utterly incredible things that have befallen the Jews in the past century resemble the fantastic tales of the Bible. In a few months Abba relives the experiences of

Abraham, of Jacob, of Jonah, and follows his ancestors through Sodom and Gomorrah, Beth-El, and the belly of the whale. Intimations of archetypal experiences haunt every moment of his escape to Rumania and then his voyage across the ocean: "Abba had little learning, but Biblical references ran through his mind . . ."(112). Destruction, exile, and flight are the inescapable matrix of Jewish historical experience, so that "Abba felt he had become his own great-great-grandfather, who had fled Chmielnitzki's pogroms . . ."(110).

Abba's Jonah-like trip across the Atlantic has been arranged by his prosperous sons who live in suburban New Jersey. The sons have, after a fashion, continued the fifteen-generations-old family tradition by operating a shoe factory. They are also, after a fashion, Jews, but so clean-shaven, so sterilized, so "reformed" that when he is brought to their synagogue, "Abba was sure he had been hauled into church to be converted . . ."(117). Abba's traumatic experiences make it hard for him to fathom that he is in New Jersey rather than the Land of Goshen. His sons and daughters-in-law nearly despair of rescuing him from the nightmare of the Jewish past until he accidentally comes upon a sack containing his shoemaker's equipment from Frampol. Work, which provides the one unfailing continuity in his life, proves to be his salvation. Once his sons provide him with a cobbler's bench and the tools of his craft, Abba returns to life.

For all Singer's wry condescension towards the Americanized imitation of the Jewish world of Eastern Europe (itself an imitation of the Holy Land), he does show the community reestablished in this new world. "On the following Sunday eight work stools were set up in the hut. Abba's sons spread sackcloth aprons on their knees and went to work, cutting soles and shaping heels, boring holes and hammering pegs, as in the good old days." "The Little Shoemakers" is one of the few Singer stories to allow for the possibility of a collective Jewish identity in the United States. For Abba and his sons survive not merely as individuals, but as a Jewish community. "No, praise God, they had not become idolaters in Egypt. They had not forgotten their heritage, nor had they lost themselves among the unworthy"(118–19). The lyrical rise of the story's end is a hymn to the Jewish power of survival which gains its special force from the fact that it is built into an elegy over a destroyed civilization.

III *Stories of Love and Perversion*

Rare indeed is the Singer story that does not deal with some aspect of love. "I am," he has said, "very much interested in the relations between man and woman. This is a topic which will never be exhausted. Every man and every woman is different. And every day the same man is a different man and the same woman is a different woman. So here we have a treasure for our imagination without end."[8] For Singer the energy of sexuality pervades everything, from the lowest (in "The Mirror" we read that "a male stone mounted a female stone") to the highest: "God Himself and all His worlds were divided into he and she, male and female, give and take, a lust that no matter how much it was satisfied . . . could never be sated completely and always wanted more, something new, different."[9]

Singer's stress upon variety and possiblity makes it difficult to ascribe to him a "philosophy" of love. Women often figure in his stories as embodiments of the sensual principle which distracts men from the life of piety or the life of intellect. But whereas in some stories (like "The Riddle") no compromise between the male who wishes to serve God and the female in bondage to her flesh is tolerated, in others the woman represents the creative principle capable of restoring life to men (like Dr. Fischelson of "The Spinoza of Market Street") in whom the springs of life have been dried up by Spinozist or other rationalisms. The materialistic and atheistic gentile Dr. Yaretzky of "The Shadow of a Crib," terrified by Schopenhauer's description of woman as a "narrow-waisted, high-breasted, wide-hipped vessel of sex, which blind will has formed for his own purposes," refuses the miracle of creative union offered him by the widow Helena and thereby condemns her and himself to sterility and death.

Sexuality, like all things originally good (and perhaps more than most), is liable to perversion if carried to excess. Nowhere in Singer's fiction is the perversion to which sexuality is liable, and the grotesque forms of which all life is capable, expressed with more force than in the story "Blood" (in *Short Friday and Other Stories*). Although, as Singer is fond of remarking, the Kabbalists attributed sex even to God, they also knew that "the passion for blood and the passion for flesh have the same origin, and this is the reason 'Thou

shalt not kill' is followed by 'Thou shalt not commit adultery.' "
"Blood" strictly illustrates, in the career of its main character Risha,
the truth of this ancient dictum.

The twice-widowed Risha has married the pious and (as his surname denotes) honest Reb Falik Ehrlichman, a man thirty years
her senior. Although endowed with the high bosom and "broad
hips" of Schopenhauer's insatiable life force, she has never borne
a child, and she never will. As her husband departs from active life
into piety and old age, Risha becomes enamored of Reuben the
butcher, precisely because of his prowess at slaughtering animals.
Reuben, though coarse, fleshy, and lecherous, is linked, as a ritual
slaughterer, with religion itself. He reminds Risha of this in his
rejection of her (pretended) pity for his victims: " 'When you scale
a fish on the Sabbath, do you think the fish enjoys it?' " (30). Within
the confines of piety itself, Singer thus slyly insinuates, there is
compulsory cruelty, a point made much more insistently in the
zealously vegetarian story "The Slaughterer," whose hero "could
not bear the sight of blood."

Risha discovers that her lust is aroused by watching Reuben
slaughter hens and roosters. At first she wishes to identify with his
victims by copulating with him: "In their amorous play, she asked
him to slaughter her. Taking her head, he bent it back and fiddled
with his finger across her throat. When Risha finally arose, she said
to Reuben: 'You certainly murdered me that time' " (33). As Risha
reduces herself more and more to the state of the human animal,
the old figure of the "beast with two backs" is literally realized, and
the panting of the lovers is both provoked by and indistinguishable
from the death-rattles of the animals in whose straw they rustle.

Having begun by identifying with the victim, Risha goes a step
further and identifies with the slaughterer himself. Although she
has studied neither the *Shulchan Aruch* nor the Commentaries
which a slaughterer is required to know, she insists on taking over
Reuben's work. As Irving Buchen points out,[10] this usurpation of
the male role is a crucial element in the growth of Risha's perversion.
But its ultimate significance lies in the fact that if you live for pleasure, you must aspire to the ultimate pleasure of murder itself.
Risha becomes dominant even over the brutal Reuben because her
killing is done solely for pleasure and cannot be confined within the
bounds of ritual. Despite his protests, therefore, she not only
slaughters animals but practices deception upon the Jewish com-

munity by slaughtering horses and pigs and selling them as kosher beef. This gives her a pleasure on a par with lechery and cruelty, and demonstrates that any single sin both invites and encompasses all the others. Sexuality, Singer shows, is not something universally to be encouraged, for among the wicked it is essentially violent. Eventually Risha and Reuben are discovered. Set upon by a mob, Reuben flees and Risha becomes a convert to Christianity. By this device she not only affords herself protection but joins those who command the weapons of slaughter and separates herself from the eternally victimized Jews. But once her husband drops dead of shock she can no longer derive any pleasure from lust and slaughter, for there is no one for her to betray and mock. Tormented in dreams by the phantoms of animals, Risha turns into a carnivorous beast, a ravening werewolf, and is at last fatally wounded by the Jews of Laskev. Despite a life of sexual abandon, despite her three husbands and her gargantuan sexual exploits with the lascivious butcher— now turned vegetarian penitent—Risha has produced nothing. It is as if the energy which in a normal woman goes into procreation cannot be inert but must, if not expended in the creation of life, work toward its destruction.

"Yentl the Yeshiva Boy" (in *Short Friday . . .*) is one of Singer's most balanced, tactful, and restrained treatments of the subject of the perversion to which even the noblest of human impulses—the disinterested pursuit of wisdom and of love—may lead. Yentl's troubles had begun when her bedridden father studied Torah with her just as if she were a boy, and she proved so apt a pupil that her whole soul yearned toward the world of Torah scholarship. But that very world had itself decreed that only men's souls could yearn toward such a consummation, whereas women were to fulfill themselves in the production and rearing of Jewish children. What reader of Yiddish literature can forget the satirical thrust of the question put by Miriam, the heroine of Peretz's "Devotion without End," to the angels of Paradise who, believing her to be a man (the husband for whom she sacrificed herself), ask her whether she studied the Torah: "She smiled charmingly: 'Lord of the Universe, have you ever directed the daughters of Israel to study your Torah?' "

"Yentl" is the kind of story that can easily be misconstrued by readers unfamiliar with Jewish life, and will almost certainly be miscontrued by Jewish readers of the feminist persuasion. Although Yentl is in many respects, including the physical, "not cut out for a woman's life," it is explicitly her desire to study Torah that propels her into the drastic decision to dress herself as a man and enter a yeshiva. For feminism, as for all the varied offspring of leftist ideology, Singer has nothing but contempt. But Yentl is treated with sympathy (partial, to be sure) because she wants equality not as a woman with men but as a Jew with other Jews.

Singer's resistance toward Yentl's ambition arises from two causes. One is his traditionalist view that Judaism depends on distinction and separation: weekday from Sabbath, gentile from Jew, meat from milk, woman from man. Therefore the story frequently endorses the wisdom of the commandment that "A woman shall not wear that which pertaineth to a man." Singer believes that far more than a sartorial preference underlies this prohibition, for Yentl's blurring of the distinction between the sexes deceives both herself and others, perverts her life, and harms everyone associated with her. Primary among her unintended victims are Avigdor, her yeshiva study partner and soul brother, and Hadass, whom Yentl (or Anshel, as she is known) actually marries.

Although Yentl-Anshel marries Hadass for the highest of motives—to recover her for Avigdor, whose fiancée she had been—she thereby entangles herself in sin and depravity. Hadass, to be sure, loves her Anshel and is so innocent that she doesn't know (and doesn't care) that she is not truly married. They are tender and loving to each other. Yet Singer never allows us to forget that whatever else may be said for homosexual relationships, they do not do much for propagation of the race and perpetuation of the Jewish people. This is the second insuperable objection to Yentl's ambition to dedicate her life to the study of Torah.

Yet Singer does not entirely withdraw his sympathy from Yentl. Even after she reveals her true identity to Avigdor, they continue to study Torah together, a scholarly David and Jonathan. "Though their bodies were different, their souls were of one kind." This being so, Yentl is quite right to reply to Avigdor's desperate suggestion that they both seek divorces in order to marry each other that " 'I wanted to study the Gemara and Commentaries with you, not darn your socks' " (154–55).

The story's practical problem is resolved by the disappearance of Yentl and the marriage of Hadass (to whom she sends divorce papers) to Avigdor. The true purpose of marriage, thwarted by homosexuality, is now fulfilled: "Not long after the wedding, Hadass became pregnant" (159). But gain must be measured against loss. What has been lost is the Torah scholar named Yentl, who by symbolic extension stands for whole generations of potential Torah scholars lost to the Jewish people through an accident of birth.[11]

IV   *Autobiographical Stories*

Increasingly during recent years, Singer has written stories that are thinly veiled segments of autobiography. In the three early collections of stories, this genre does not appear. In the fourth volume, *The Seance*, we have one story, "The Lecture," that is distinctly in Singer's autobiographical voice. In the fifth collection, *A Friend of Kafka*, a number of obviously autobiographical tales appear, among them "Guests on a Winter Night," "Dr. Beeber," "The Mentor," "Schloimele," and "The Son," a story that touches on the painful subject of Singer's meeting, after a separation of twenty years, with the son he had by his first wife. By the time of *A Crown of Feathers* (1973) autobiographical tales predominate.

In some of these stories the imaginative pressure is very low, and the distinction between fiction and memoir nearly invisible. In others—and these are not only the more interesting but also the ones which tell us more about their author—the narrator places himself midway between the real Isaac Bashevis Singer and a number of imagined voices and personae which dramatize the conflicting impulses of Singer's inner world or draw out into extreme form principles and ideas we know to have been held by the author himself. A convenient way of suggesting the range of the autobiographical stories is to glance at a few of the many tales which deal with Singer's career as a Yiddish writer and, therefore, with the fate of Yiddish itself in the aftermath of the Holocaust.

"A Day in Coney Island," although published as a story along with the others that make up *A Crown of Feathers*, could just as easily function as straight autobiographical writing. The story tells of a thirty-year-old Yiddish writer from Poland who fears that, because he has only a tourist visa, he will be deported to the land of his birth and there fall victim to Hitler. Although the editor of a Yiddish paper has published a few of his stories, he has also complained that no one in America "gave a hoot about demons, dybbuks, and imps of two hundred years ago." The narrator was, he recalls, himself afflicted by doubts and by the fear that at age thirty he was already an anachronism. " 'Who needs Yiddish in America?' I asked myself" (31). As in virtually all of Singer's autobiographical memoirs of the thirties, there is much worrying over whether it is permissible to marry someone just to obtain a visa. Although the story's narrator practices ironic self-depreciation—referring frequently to the ir-relevance of a writer who dwells, and in Yiddish, on werewolves, sprites, and other themes " 'no one cares about and nobody believes in' "—our knowledge of the fact that the narrator is none other than Singer himself, who has gained a world reputation, fame and fortune and a Nobel Prize, for writing of such irrelevancies, does much to offset this impression of modesty.

"The Lecture" is an autobiographical tale with far greater range and resonance than "A Day in Coney Island." Singer has lectured so widely (probably in every American state as well as Canada, Latin America, and Israel) that it is hardly surprising that his stories about occurrences on his lecture tours virtually constitute a subgroup in themselves. The story is told by a famous Yiddish writer called "N." who has traveled by train from New York to Montreal in order to deliver what must have been an intriguing lecture, for it is "an optimistic report on the future of the Yiddish language" (65). But we never learn more of the lecture than that it "predicted a brilliant future for Yiddish" (66) because a snowstorm slows the train and makes the writer late for his appearance. In any case, he later loses the manuscript, a mishap which does not entirely dis-please him because it means that "people will hear fewer lies" (70) and that he will not have to bear the burden of explaining how it is that Yiddish can have a bright future when all empirical evidence suggests its imminent demise.

Here again the author indulges in a wry and ironic depreciation of himself in his character as a writer in a dead, or at least a dying, language. But the center of the story is more sombre still, for what it says about the Yiddish writer is that everything draws him back to the subject of the Holocaust, and that for him artistic detachment is an impossibility. The problem of the Yiddish writer is not the future, but the past. The only two members of the Montreal Jewish society willing to brave the storm in order to collect Mr. N. at the station at two-thirty in the morning are a loquacious survivor of the death camps and her daughter. So lame that she can barely walk, the older woman has risked her life in order to welcome her favorite writer, whose stories had lifted some of the darkness from her heart when she first read them in the DP camps after the war. After such a tribute, and in view of the lateness of the hour, Mr. N. can hardly refuse the invitation to spend the night at the apartment of these two women.

He quickly discovers that it is only physically that this old, crippled woman lives in Montreal. Her mental life is among the murdered, who include her three sons. In fact, she has even carried her old ambience to the New World. The street where she lives reminds Mr. N. of a small town in Poland—murky, narrow, lined with wooden houses. The apartment is shabby, icy, and filled with the smells of that dead world. "In some mysterious way the mother and daughter had managed to bring with them the whole atmosphere of wretched poverty from their old home in Poland" (74). It is precisely at the point where he has assimilated all this that the writer discovers the loss of his manuscript. He aptly describes it as a "Freudian" accident, for it pointedly tells him that Yiddish is now irrevocably bound not merely to the Jewish past but to the destroyed world of East European Jewry. Yiddish literature is kept from artistic freedom, or perhaps saved from artistic irresponsibility, by the immediacy of the Yiddish writer's involvement with the uniquely terrible fate of modern Jewry. Giving up his manuscript for lost, Mr. N., suffering from the iciness of his room, tries by an act of imaginative sympathy to place himself in the Holocaust world of his two hostesses: "Let me imagine that I had remained under Hitler in wartime. Let me get some taste of that, too. . . . I imagined myself somewhere in Treblinka or Maidanek. I had done hard labor all day long. . . . Tomorrow there would probably be a 'selection,' and since I was no longer well, I would be sent to the ovens. . ." (77). Mr. N. now sounds much like the Singer who prefaces *Enemies* with the remark that "I did not have the privilege of going through the Hitler holocaust."

But it turns out that this Yiddish writer need not strain to find the realm of misfortune, for he is awakened from his dream by the daughter's frenzied report of her mother's sudden death. The old woman has in fact been killed by the strain of coming out in the snow to meet the revered writer, who now has a corpse on his hands. The macabre, surrealistic, and even gruesome tendencies of this tale are now given full play. Mr. N.—very much like the *shlimazel* of Sholom Aleichem's famous story "Eternal Life"—finds himself afflicted by the very thing he had most feared since boyhood:

being alone with a corpse in the dark. The recrudescence of this boyhood terror completes the process whereby all of N.'s decades of life in the United States are shown to be insubstantial and unreal, capable of being dispelled by any crisis which wrenches literature back to the source from whence it derives. "My years in America seemed to have been swept away by that one night and I was taken back, as though by magic, to my worst days in Poland. . ." (81).

There is yet a third kind of autobiographical tale in which Singer explores the ambiguous relationship between the modern Yiddish writer and the experience of modern Jewry. "A Day in Coney Island" exemplifies Singer's realistic approach to this subject, "The Lecture" his surrealistic one, and "The Last Demon" (in *Short Friday* . . .) what might tentatively be called his supernatural one. Of the many stories in which Singer uses a first-person narrator who bears marked resemblances to the author, none comes so close to representing his inner relationship to his own work as this one. The narrator tells of his plight as the last remaining demon, whose occupation is gone because man himself has become a demon: to proselytize for evil in these times would be carrying coals to Newcastle. Like Singer himself, the last demon has been deprived of his subject, the Jews of Eastern Europe. "I've seen it all," he says, "the destruction of Tishevitz, the destruction of Poland. There are no more Jews, no more demons. . . . The community was slaughtered, the holy books burned, the cemetery desecrated." Like Singer the last demon attempts to speak as if history had *not* destroyed his subject and as if he could defy time: "I speak in the present tense as for me time stands still" (120). Like Singer, the last demon knows, or thinks he knows, that there is no judge and no judgment, and that to the generation which has indeed succeeded in becoming wholly guilty the only Messiah that will come is death: "The generation is already guilty seven times over, but Messiah does not come. To whom should he come? Messiah did not come for the Jews, so the Jews went to Messiah" (129). Like Singer, finally, the demon must sustain himself on dust and ashes and Yiddish books. "I found a Yiddish storybook between two broken barrels in the house which once belonged to Velvel the Barrelmaker. I sit there, the last of the demons. I eat dust. . . . The style of the book is . . . Sabbath pudding cooked in pig's fat: blasphemy rolled in piety. The moral of the book is: neither judge, nor judgment. But nevertheless the letters are Jewish. . . . I suck on the letters and feed myself. . . . Yes, as long as a single volume remains, I have something to sustain me" (130).

V Gimpel the Fool

"Gimpel the Fool" (in *Gimpel the Fool* . . .) is without question Singer's best-known, most frequently anthologized, and most thoroughly studied short story. When Saul Bellow's translation of it appeared in *Partisan Review* in 1953, the barrier of parochialism which has kept the American literary world ignorant of even the greatest of Yiddish writers in the United States was lowered long enough for Singer to make his escape from the cage of Yiddish into the outside world. But even those critics who, like the Shakespeare scholar Paul Siegel, have located Gimpel, as the wise or sainted fool, within the most pervasive archetypes of Western literature, have admitted that he is inescapably of the Yiddish world, and that the story "has its roots deep in the soil of Yiddish literature."[12] Irving Howe explicitly labels him "the literary grandson of Peretz's Bontsha Schweig, whose intolerable humbleness makes even the angels in heaven feel guilty and embarrassed," although he reminds us that the activist Peretz did not, like Singer, endorse schlemielhood.[13]

What mainly characterizes Gimpel is his readiness to believe everything he is told, no matter how improbable, fantastic, "incredible." He is fooled into playing truant from school by being told the lie that the rabbi's wife has been brought to child-bed. When his tormentors found out how credulous he was, they gave free rein to their imagination in lies: " 'Gimpel, the Czar is coming to Frampol; Gimpel, the moon fell down in Turbeen. . . .' And I like a *golem* believed everyone." He believed, he says, because traditional wisdom conveyed the awareness that "everything is possible" (4), awareness that, since the time of the Holocaust, has been alleged by historians to be the peculiar advantage of the criminal mind over the noncriminal.

Sometimes the tricks played on poor Gimpel touched on the most sacred things or on those by which a human being is most immediately attached to life. Told that the Messiah has come and the dead, including his own mother and father, have arisen from the grave, he runs outside to look, even though he "knew very well that nothing of the sort had happened." Shamed by the howls of laughter

which mock his (apparent) credulity, he momentarily resolves "to
believe nothing more." But the rabbi reassures him, not—as perhaps he ought to have done—with the reminder that a believing
Jew can hardly be superior and sceptical about that Messianic deliverance towards which his whole religion yearns, but on moral
grounds. " 'It is written, better to be a fool all your days than for
one hour to be evil. . . . For he who causes his neighbor to feel
shame loses Paradise himself' " (5).

The central foolishness of Gimpel's life is the willingness with
which he allows himelf to be duped (or is he?) into marrying Elka,
who is (and whom Gimpel knows to be, though he is told otherwise)
the town whore. She is a widow, she is divorced, and she is pregnant
with a bastard who is born seventeen weeks after the wedding with
Gimpel. He accepts the child as his own, only to be subjected to
the further humiliation of finding Elka in bed with another man.
At first he refuses to credit (or pretend to credit) her lies, saying
that " 'Gimpel isn't going to be a sucker all his life. There's a limit
even to the foolishness of a fool like Gimpel' " (11). But two impulses
keep him from asserting his dignity—and his incredulity. One is his
incapacity for righteous anger and hatred, an incapacity that some
writers on the Holocaust have found widespread among the Jews
of Eastern Europe. The other is his instinctive sense that belief is
not a matter of evidences but of will. This is Gimpel's positive
version of that favorite negative doctrine of dogmatic thinkers:
namely, that those who deny speculative truths are morally at fault,
and that, as the Catholic thinker John Henry Newman once wrote
to a prospective convert to his faith, *"We can believe what we
choose."*[14]

This link, on the surface utterly absurd, between faith in one's
(unfaithful) wife, and faith in God is made by Gimpel himself and
does not depend on the reader's inference. "All Frampol refreshed
its spirits because of my trouble and grief. However, I resolved that
I would always believe what I was told. What's the good of *not*
believing? Today it's your wife you don't believe; tomorrow it's God
Himself you won't take stock in" (14). Gimpel never takes the analogy a step further to say that the Jewish people have been far more
faithful to their God than He to them, but in the aftermath of the
Holocaust there are few Jewish heads through which that thought
will not at least momentarily flit when they read this passage.

Elka's continuing infidelities over two decades do try Gimpel's

love and faith, but his belief in belief itself is strong enough to blot
out all negative empirical evidence. "All kinds of things happened,
but I neither saw nor heard. I believed, and that's all. The rabbi
recently said to me, 'Belief in itself is beneficial. It is written that
a good man lives by his faith' " (17). Gimpel's last temptation is
proffered by Satan himself, who after Elka's deathbed confession
of her lifelong deception of Gimpel suggests that he get even with
all the inhabitants of Frampol by pouring urine in the dough of
their bread. But just as Gimpel is about to risk eternal life for a
dirty act of revenge, God comes to his aid by sending a message
through Elka, who appears in a dream to say to Gimpel: " 'Because
I was false is everything false too?' " (19). This is God's way of
keeping faith with Gimpel when his belief in his wife, the foundation
on which all other beliefs had rested, crumbles. For the rest of the
story, Gimpel wanders through the world as a storyteller in his own
right, a sage who spins yarns about "improbable things that could
never have happened" (20).

Despite Gimpel's descent from the schlemiels of the classical
Yiddish writers, he differs from them in several respects. Unlike
Sholom Aleichem's Kasrilevkites or Peretz's Bontsha, he *chooses*
to be fooled, to be used, to forsake his dignity. This means that not
only his creator but he himself is capable of irony about the sacrifices
required by faith. Also, his folly is connected with his credulity,
whereas much of the folly of his Yiddish predecessors comes precisely from their unwillingness to credit unusual and extraordinary
events, especially if these portend evil. Thus, the crucial moment
of Sholom Aleichem's "Dreyfus in Kasrilevke" comes when the lone
newspaper subscriber in town reads to the citizens the news of
Alfred Dreyfus's unjust conviction for treason against France. They
react in violent protest, "not against the judge who had judged so
badly . . . not against the generals who had sworn so falsely nor
against the Frenchmen who had covered themselves with so much
shame," but against Zaidle, who reads them the news. " 'If you
stood here with one foot in heaven and one foot on earth we still
wouldn't believe you. Such things cannot be! No, this cannot be!
It cannot be! It cannot be!' " It is true that this incredulity of the
Kasrilevkites is connected causally with their faith that divine truth
and justice must prevail, yet it goes without saying that Gimpel in
the same situation would at once have credited the grim news from
France.

All this should be kept in mind when considering Ruth Wisse's suggestion that, in a sense, the most important fact about this story is its postwar date of composition. "How," she asks, "does one retain the notion of psychic survival when its cost has been physical extinction? . . . After the entire populations of Kasrilevke and Tuneyadevke have been reduced to the ash of crematoria, does it not become a cruel sentimentality to indulge in schlemiel humor and to sustain a faith in the ironic mode?" Singer's story, she points out, is one of the rare examples in postwar Yiddish fiction of the schlemiel figure, whose development is the subject of her book. She suggests, without insisting on, the possible link between the traditional celebration of the schlemiel's innocence or gullibility, and the inability or refusal of the majority of Jews "to face reality" when they were being herded into ghettoes, concentration camps, and finally gas chambers.[15] She accepts the tradition (bitterly repudiated by survivors like Alexander Donat)[16] that the hymn of the camps was *Ani Maamin* (I believe) and implies the link with Gimpel's celebration of belief against all evidence.

But was it really their religious faith that made the majority of Jews disbelieve in the actuality of the threat which faced them? Most witnesses and survivors have alleged that, on the contrary, it was their faith in "mankind" and in the "world" which betrayed the majority of Jews. If that is so, then we can accept "Gimpel the Fool" as a story written not in spite of, but because of, Singer's awareness of the Holocaust. If worldliness is indeed the gullibility which disbelieves everything, then this is the most intense of all Singer's assaults upon it, for Gimpel is a character who insists on believing everything. He is sternly indifferent to the voice of common sense, that faculty which, according to Hannah Arendt, because it encouraged them "to explain away the intrinsically incredible by means of liberal rationalizations,"[17] was the most fatal of all to the appointed victims of the Holocaust. If, Gimpel might say, you disbelieve the nations who threaten to remove the Jewish people from the face of the earth, you will disbelieve anything.

CHAPTER 10

Conclusion

A CCORDING to Irving Howe, the most important single fact about Isaac Bashevis Singer is that "no other living writer has yielded himself so completely and recklessly . . . to the claims of the human imagination."[1] That is to say, he has devoted his life to writing about a world that was brutally destroyed, and has done so in a language that is itself on the verge of extinction. Singer's work takes it entirely for granted that the only subject worth writing about is the Jewish people who were destroyed solely for the "crime" of having been born. What he writes about, however, is not their destruction but their life; they survive through the grace of his creative imagination.

Only a few decades ago, Yiddish was the language of the Jewish masses, spoken by about eleven million people. Now, in the wake of the Holocaust and the Soviet onslaught against Yiddish culture and the disintegration of immigrant Jewish culture in the United States, it has become the language of a tiny, beleaguered coterie. In one sense, then, Singer's work would seem to be the culminating but also the final achievement of Yiddish literature. But we must remember that for the majority of his readers Singer exists in translation, not only in the linguistic sense—from Yiddish to English— but from the culture of Old World Judaism to the internalized "Jewishness" of American Jewry. If what Cynthia Ozick calls "New Yiddish"—a literature "which is centrally Jewish in its concerns and thereby liturgical in nature"[2]—should come into being, then Singer may one day be viewed not as the last great figure of a destroyed culture but as the harbinger of a new Jewish literature.

Yet it goes without saying that any literary forecast which assumes the continuance of Jewish life anywhere in the world is hazardous. Nazism let loose against the Jews a primordial energy of destructiveness which has by no means spent itself. The oldest Jewish communities of forty years ago—in Germany, in Poland, in Yemen, in Iraq—today are no more. Jewish life is shrinking everywhere in the Diaspora. The state of Israel, the last remaining center of the historic Jewish civilization, has become a pariah nation, whose reduction to sandy wastes seems to be the primary *desideratum* of what is politely still called the family of nations. "There is," says the philosopher Joseph Dan, "no reason whatsoever to expect that the twentieth century will treat Jews any better in its concluding quarter than it did during its second and third quarters."[3]

That Singer's work will survive, we can hardly doubt. But whether it will survive as part of a living culture or as a splendid relic of "the glory that was Israel," a peg for liberal theology to hang pieties on, depends on the fate of the Jews themselves.

Notes and References

Chapter One

1. *In My Father's Court* (New York, 1966), p. 68.
2. "On Living in the Gentile World," in *Modern Jewish Thought: A Source Reader*, ed. Nahum N. Glatzer (New York, 1977), p. 172.
3. *In My Father's Court*, p. 51.
4. Joel Blocker and Richard Elman, "An Interview with Isaac Bashevis Singer," in *Critical Views of Isaac Bashevis Singer*, ed. Irving Malin (New York, 1969), pp. 15–16.
5. *In My Father's Court*, p. 171.
6. Ibid., p. 77.
7. Ibid., p. 154.
8. Ibid., p. 155.
9. Ibid., p. 207.
10. Ibid., pp. 239–40.
11. Ibid., p. 240.
12. Ibid., p. 188.
13. Ibid., p. 287.
14. Ibid., pp. 289–90.
15. *A Young Man in Search of Love* (New York, 1978), p. 107.
16. Ibid., p. 161.
17. *A Treasury of Yiddish Stories* (New York, 1953), p. 25.
18. *Critical Views of Isaac Bashevis Singer*, p. 16.
19. Morton A. Reichek, "Storyteller," *New York Times Magazine*, March 23, 1975, p. 26.
20. "Yiddish, The Language of Exile," *Judaica Book News* (Spring/Summer 1976), p. 27.

Chapter Two

1. Gershom Scholem, *The Messianic Idea in Judaism* (New York, 1971), p. 60.
2. Ibid., p. 61.

3. Ibid., p. 94.

4. Ibid., pp. 88–89.

5. The fact that Rechele can be freed of evil influences only at the price of death would seem to confute the otherwise plausible and helpful theory of Professor Irving Buchen that "her life and fate become the record not only of the Jews of Goray in the seventeenth century, but also of the entire Jewish people before and after that nexus."—*Isaac Bashevis Singer and the Eternal Past* (New York, 1968), p. 96.

6. *Critical Views of Isaac Bashevis Singer*, ed. Irving Malin (New York, 1969), p. 15.

7. *The Messianic Idea in Judaism*, p. 7.

8. Moshe Flinker, *Young Moshe's Diary* (Jerusalem, 1971), pp. 28–29, 55.

Chapter Three

1. Abraham Joshua Heschel, *Between God and Man*, ed. Fritz A. Rothschild (New York, 1959), p. 217.

2. Bernard Lazare, *Job's Dungheap* (New York, 1948), p. 97.

3. *Peretz*, ed. and trans. Sol Liptzin (New York, 1947), p. 18.

4. Hannah Arendt, *The Origins of Totalitarianism*, 3 vols. (New York, 1951), I, 120.

5. See, in this connection, the letter of Moses Leib Lilienblum to J. L. Gordon in *The Golden Tradition*, ed. Lucy S. Dawidowicz (Boston, 1968), pp. 127–29.

6. Quoted in *The Golden Tradition*, p. 50.

7. J. L. Talmon, "European History as the Seedbed of the Holocaust," in *Holocaust and Rebirth: A Symposium* (Jerusalem, 1974), p. 70. This is not Talmon's own view, but his caricature of the historicist view.

8. Irving Saposnik, in a vigorous and intelligent (although, in my view, ultimately mistaken) article entitled "Translating the Family Moskat" (*Yiddish*, I [Fall 1973], 26–37), has compared the differing implications of the English and Yiddish endings of the novel. He argues that whereas "the English text ends in confusion," the Yiddish concludes with an affirmation consonant with the character of the whole of the original version, which is a "tribute to the endurance of European Jewry." Saposnik believes that all changes from the Yiddish to the English version derive from Singer's sense that the English-speaking audience is better attuned to what he calls the nihilistic note on which the novel ends. This is especially the case, he contends, with the book's ending: "The omission of the final chapter, with its evidence of spiritual regeneration, turned the novel away from its traditional roots toward exactly that fragmented modernism that the original transcended" (p. 27). Saposnik attaches great importance to the original ending, spoken by Asa: " 'These words [the Decalogue] weren't unclear

and devoid of meaning. The Nazi couldn't weaken this. These weren't words but flames that the Eternal Jew threw out against the Eternal Villains.' "

The reasons why Saposnik attaches exaggerated importance to the different endings are several: first, his belief that Asa is the book's hero in the traditional sense; second, his conclusion that Singer is guilty, in the English text, of "a systematic exclusion of the numerous references to the messianic faith of Judaism"; third, his ascription to Singer of his own view that the ultimate triumph of Zionism vindicates the messianic expectations portrayed in the book.

Chapter Four

1. Yasha's insistence upon the instinctive, unconscious nature of his gift—" 'Does the spider know how it spins its web?' "—strongly resembles Singer's published statements on the creative gift of the writer. "When you ask a writer what he meant by his story it's like asking a chicken which lays an egg what chemicals did she use to lay this egg."—"Isaac Bashevis Singer: Conversation in California," *Modern Fiction Studies*, XVI (Winter 1970–71), 434.

2. Irving Howe, *Politics and the Novel* (New York, 1957), p. 144.

3. Of Judaism's inability to assimilate Western European culture without destroying itself, we have abundant evidence. See, for example, the striking excerpt from the memoirs of that brilliant observer of Jewish life Pauline Wengeroff in Lucy Dawidowicz, *The Golden Tradition*, pp. 160–68.

Chapter Five

1. Celia S. Heller, *On the Edge of Destruction: Jews of Poland between the Two World Wars* (New York, 1977), p. 15.

Chapter Six

1. John Thompson, "Stories about Terrible Things," *Commentary*, XLIV (December 1967), 79.

2. Introduction to *The Jewish Expression* (New York, 1970), pp. xiv–xv.

3. *In Praise of Yiddish* (New York, 1971), p. 114.

4. Mary Ellmann, "The Piety of Things in *The Manor*," in *The Achievement of Isaac Bashevis Singer*, ed. Marcia Allentuck (Carbondale, Ill., 1969), p. 125.

5. Ibid., p. 134.

6. Ibid., p. 135.

7. Hillel Halkin, *Letters to an American Jewish Friend* (Philadelphia, 1977), p. 182.

8. See Celia S. Heller, *On the Edge of Destruction: Jews of Poland Between the Two World Wars* (New York, 1977).

9. Martin Buber makes this distinction. See *The Writings of Martin Buber*, ed. Will Herberg (New York, 1956), p. 281.

Chapter Seven

1. Irving Howe, Introduction to *Selected Short Stories of Isaac Bashevis Singer* (New York, 1966), p. vii.

2. Yehuda Bauer, Leni Yahil, and Joseph Litvak, "Rescue," in *Holocaust* (Jerusalem, 1974), p. 124.

3. See Yehuda Bauer, *The Holocaust in Historical Perspective* (Seattle, 1978), pp. 30–36.

4. "Reflections on the Possibility of Jewish Mysticism in Our Time," *Ariel*, XXVI (Spring 1970), 46.

5. Emil L. Fackenheim, "The Voice of Auschwitz," in *Modern Jewish Thought*, ed. Nahum N. Glatzer, pp. 188–89.

Chapter Eight

1. Singer's first novel written in the first person was *A Ship to America*, serialized in the *Forward* in 1958.

2. Cynthia Ozick, "Notes toward a Meditation on 'Forgiveness,' " in Simon Wiesenthal, *The Sunflower* (New York, 1976), p. 185.

3. Irving Buchen has identified "the dilemma of the intelligent woman in the man-dominated world of traditional Judaism" as one of Singer's favorite themes. —*Isaac Bashevis Singer and the Eternal Past*, p. 122. Singer's story "Yentl the Yeshiva Boy," to be discussed later, deals with a girl like the Ludmir Maiden, and his play of the same name ran for three weeks in an off-Broadway theater.

Chapter Nine

1. Irving Howe, Introduction to *Selected Short Stories of Isaac Bashevis Singer* (New York, 1966), pp. xvi, xii.

2. "America: Toward Yavneh," *Judaism*, XIX (Summer 1970), 275.

3. Morton A. Reichek, "Storyteller," *New York Times Magazine*, March 23, 1975, p. 28.

4. Quoted in Howe, Introduction to *Selected Short Stories of Isaac Bashevis Singer*, p. xi.

5. See, on this subject, Edward Alexander, "The Incredibility of the Holocaust," in *The Resonance of Dust: Essays on Holocaust Literature and Jewish Fate* (Columbus, Ohio, 1979).

6. Morris Golden, "Dr. Fischelson's Miracle: Duality and Vision in Sing-

er's Fiction," in *The Achievement of Isaac Bashevis Singer*, ed. Marcia Allentuck (Carbondale, Ill., 1969).

7. Introduction to *A Treasury of Yiddish Stories* (New York, 1953), p. 86.

8. Reichek, "Storyteller," p. 22.

9. *A Young Man in Search of Love* (New York, 1978), p. 135.

10. Irving Buchen, *Isaac Bashevis Singer and the Eternal Past* (New York, 1968), p. 121.

11. See, on this subject, Cynthia Ozick, "The Jewish Half-Genius," *Jerusalem Post International Edition*, August 8, 1978, pp. 10–11.

12. "Gimpel and the Archetype of the Wise Fool," in *The Achievement of Isaac Bashevis Singer*, p. 159.

13. Introduction to *A Treasury of Yiddish Stories*, p. 41.

14. *The Letters and Diaries of John Henry Newman*, ed. C. S. Dessain (Birmingham, 1962), XII, 228.

15. *The Schlemiel as Modern Hero* (Chicago, 1971), pp. 60–67.

16. See "The Voice of the Ashes," lecture at "The Holocaust—A Generation After" conference, New York, March 1975, to be published by Institute of Contemporary Jewry.

17. *The Origins of Totalitarianism*, 3 vols. (New York, 1951), III, 137–38.

Chapter Ten

1. Introduction to *Selected Short Stories of Isaac Bashevis Singer* (New York, 1966), p. vi.

2. "America: Toward Yavneh," *Judaism*, XIX (Summer 1970), 279.

3. "Will the Jewish People Exist in the 21st Century?" *Forum*, XXIII (Spring 1975), 61.

Glossary

Chanukah: holiday celebrating rededication of the Temple in Jerusalem in 165 B.C.E.

Chasidim: religious enthusiasts, devotees of *Chasidism* or "pietism," a religious revival beginning in the eighteenth century

dybbuk: a condemned spirit who inhabits the body of a living person and controls his actions

Eretz Israel: the Land of Israel

Gemara: section of the Talmud interpreting the *Mishnah*

goy: a Gentile, a non-Jew

halachah: that part of Jewish literature which deals with religious, ethical, civil, and criminal law

maskil: a devotee of the *Haskalah,* or Enlightenment

mezuzah: ritual object posted on the door of a Jewish home; it consists of a small parchment on which portions of the Pentateuch are inscribed, enclosed in a small container

Mishnah: earliest codification of the oral Law, which is the basis of the Talmud

Passover: festival of unleavened bread commemorating the exodus of the children of Israel from Egypt

Purim: holiday commemorating deliverance of Jews of Persia from extermination, as told in biblical Book of Esther

rebbetsin: wife of rabbi or teacher

schlemiel: a foolish and powerless but sometimes also wise and saintly individual

Shevuot: Feast of the Pentecost; festival commemorating the giving of the Torah to Moses

shtetl: Jewish town or village of Eastern Europe

Shulchan Aruch: "Prepared Table," standard code of Jewish law compiled by Joseph Karo and first published in 1565

Simchat Torah: Rejoicing of the Law; a holiday celebration

Tisha B'Av: ninth day of the month of Av; fast day commemorating destruction of the Temple in Jerusalem

Torah: narrowly, Pentateuch, but by extension all Jewish teaching

Yom Kippur: Day of Atonement

Selected Bibliography

1. Novels

Satan in Goray. Trans. Jacob Sloan. New York: Noonday Press, 1955. Originally published in Yiddish in 1934–35.

The Family Moskat. Trans. A.H. Gross. New York: Alfred A. Knopf, 1950. Yiddish publication same year.

The Magician of Lublin. Trans. Elaine Gottlieb and Joseph Singer. New York: Noonday Press, 1960. Published serially in Yiddish in the *Jewish Daily Forward* in 1959.

The Slave. Trans. I. B. Singer and Cecil Hemley. New York: Farrar, Straus & Giroux, 1962. Published serially in Yiddish in the *Forward* in 1961.

The Manor. Trans. Elaine Gottlieb and Joseph Singer. New York: Farrar, Straus & Giroux, 1967. Published serially in Yiddish in the *Forward* from 1953 to 1955.

The Estate. Trans. Joseph Singer, Elaine Gottlieb, and Elizabeth Shub. New York: Farrar, Straus & Giroux, 1969. A continuation of the work first published serially in Yiddish in the *Forward* from 1953 to 1955.

Enemies, A Love Story. Trans. Aliza Shevrin and Elizabeth Shub. New York: Farrar, Straus & Giroux, 1972. Published serially in Yiddish in the *Forward* in 1966.

Shosha. Trans. Joseph Singer. New York: Farrar, Straus & Giroux, 1978. Published serially in Yiddish in the *Forward* in 1974.

2. Collections of Short Stories

Gimpel the Fool and Other Stories. New York: Noonday Press, 1957.

The Spinoza of Market Street. New York: Farrar, Straus & Giroux, 1961.

Short Friday and Other Stories. New York, Farrar, Straus & Giroux, 1964.

The Seance and Other Stories. New York: Farrar, Straus & Giroux, 1968.

A Friend of Kafka and Other Stories. New York: Farrar, Straus & Giroux, 1970.

A Crown of Feathers and Other Stories. New York: Farrar, Straus & Giroux, 1973.

Old Love and Other Stories. New York: Farrar, Straus & Giroux, 1979.

Passions and Other Stories. New York: Farrar, Straus & Giroux, 1975.

3. Memoirs

In My Father's Court. Trans. C. Kleinerman-Goldstein, Elaine Gottlieb, and Joseph Singer. New York: Farrar, Straus & Giroux, 1966. Originally published in Yiddish in 1956.

A Little Boy in Search of God. Trans. Joseph Singer. New York: Doubleday, 1976.

A Young Man in Search of Love. Trans. Joseph Singer. New York: Doubleday, 1978.

4. Children's Books

Zlateh the Goat and Other Stories. New York: Harper & Row, 1966.

The Fearsome Inn. New York: Scribner's, 1967.

Mazel and Shlimazel, or the Milk of a Lioness. New York: Farrar, Straus & Giroux, 1967.

When Shlemiel Went to Warsaw and Other Stories. New York: Farrar, Straus and Giroux, 1968.

Joseph and Koza, or The Sacrifice to the Vistula. New York: Farrar, Straus and Giroux, 1970.

Elijah the Slave. New York: Farrar, Straus and Giroux, 1970.

Alone in the Wild Forest. New York: Farrar, Straus and Giroux, 1971.

The Wicked City. New York: Farrar, Straus and Giroux, 1972.

The Fools of Chelm and Their History. New York: Farrar, Straus and Giroux, 1973.

Why Noah Chose the Dove. New York: Farrar, Straus and Giroux, 1974.

A Tale of Three Wishes. New York: Farrar, Straus and Giroux, 1976.

Naftali the Storyteller and His Horse. New York: Farrar, Straus and Giroux, 1976.

SECONDARY SOURCES

1. Works about Singer

ALEXANDER, EDWARD. "The Destruction and Resurrection of the Jews in the Fiction of I. B. Singer." *The Resonance of Dust: Essays on Holocaust Literature and Jewish Fate.* Columbus: Ohio State University Press, 1979. Studies Singer's fictional treatment of the Holocaust.

BUCHEN, IRVING. *Isaac Bashevis Singer and the Eternal Past.* New York: New York University Press, 1968. Earliest book-length study of Singer, first-rate in scholarship as well as criticism.

Critical Views of Isaac Bashevis Singer, ed. Irving Malin. New York: New York University Press, 1969. Useful collection of critical essays, interviews, and an excellent bibliography.

ELLMANN, MARY. "The Piety of Things in *The Manor.*" *The Achievement of Isaac Bashevis Singer,* ed. Marcia Allentuck. Carbondale: Southern Illinois University Press, 1969. One of the best essays on Singer, and one of the few to recognize his religious dimension.

GLATSTEIN, JACOB. "The Fame of Bashevis Singer." *Congress Bi-Weekly,* XXXII (December 27, 1965), 17–19. The great (but little-known) Yid-

dish poet reflects acerbically on the significance of his rival's fame "in
the stranger's world," on his "horror and eroticism," on his "drab
stylelessness."

HOWE, IRVING. Introduction to *Selected Short Stories of Isaac Bashevis
Singer.* New York: The Modern Library, 1966. Best introduction to
the short stories.

KRESH, PAUL. *Isaac Bashevis Singer.* New York: Dial Press, 1979. The
first biography of Singer.

MALIN, IRVING. *Isaac Bashevis Singer.* New York: Ungar, 1972. Biographical approach to Singer's work.

OZICK, CYNTHIA. "Envy; or, Yiddish in America." *Commentary,* XLVIII
(November 1969), 33–53. Important and brilliant short story based in
part on the Yiddish literary world's resentment of Singer's success
(reprinted in *The Pagan Rabbi and Other Stories*).

SAPOSNIK, IRVING. "Translating *The Family Moskat.*" *Yiddish,* I (Fall 1973),
26–37. Important article, not only on the novel, but on Singer's con-
ception of himself as a Yiddish writer publishing in English.

SHMERUK, KHONE. Introduction to *Der shpigl un andere dertseylungen*
(The Mirror and Other Stories). Jerusalem: Hebrew University Press,
1975. Provides useful background on Singer's first-person narratives.

SIEGEL, BEN. *Isaac Bashevis Singer.* Minneapolis: University of Minnesota
Press, 1969. Brisk survey of Singer's work in Minnesota series of pam-
phlets on American writers.

2.   Works on Yiddish Literature and Eastern European Jewish Life

DAWIDOWICZ, LUCY S. *The Golden Tradition: Jewish Life and Thought
in Eastern Europe.* Boston: Beacon Press, 1967. A superb book, bril-
liantly illuminating the world which is Singer's subject.

HELLER, CELIA S. *On the Edge of Destruction: Jews of Poland between
the Two World Wars.* New York: Columbia University Press, 1977.
Intelligent, well-written sociohistorical study of pre-Holocaust Polish
Jewry.

HOWE, IRVING, and GREENBERG ELIEZER, eds. *A Treasury of Yiddish Stories.*
New York: Viking Press, 1953. Excellent introduction virtually in-
dispensable for understanding Yiddish Literature.

OZICK, CYNTHIA. "America: Toward Yavneh." *Judaism,* XIX (Summer
1970), 264–82. Important essay on the possibility of Jewish cultural
survival in the Diaspora.

SAMUEL, MAURICE. *In Praise of Yiddish.* New York: Cowles, 1971. Witty
and also learned attempt to convey to the English reader the spirit of
the Yiddish language.

WISSE, RUTH R. *The Schlemiel as Modern Hero.* Chicago: University of
Chicago Press, 1971. Articulate, intelligent history of an archetypal
figure of Yiddish writing.

Index